The Making of the Creeds

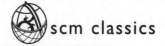

scm classics

The Making of
the Creeds

Frances M. Young

scm press

British Library Cataloguing in Publication data

A catalogue record for this book is available
from the British Library

ISBN 978 0 334 02876 5

First published in 1991 by SCM Press
13–17 Long Lane, London EC1A 9PN
This new edition published in 2002
Third Impression 2010

Typeset by Rowland Phototypesetting Ltd,
Bury St Edmunds, Suffolk
Printed by Norhaven A/S, Viborg, Denmark

Contents

Preface

One of the best things that Linda Foster achieved during her time at SCM Press was to have the idea of producing an updated version of Alan Richardson's *Creeds in the Making*. To John Bowden's eternal credit, not only did he jump at the opportunity, but he also found just the right person for the job: Frances Young, the Edward Cadbury Professor of Theology in the University of Birmingham. Now Alex Wright has recognized all that hard work of ten years and more ago by including *The Making of the Creeds* in the SCM Classics list. Why?

The simple answer is that it is a marvellous book, the finest introduction to any area of Christian theology published in the 1990s. Frances Young was able to take the strongest qualities of Richardson's original – its passion, clarity and scholarship – and pass them through the lens of contemporary intellectual debate. Young thereby added an extra layer of sophistication to the story of the development of Christian doctrine, an addition that caught the cool beauty of the early Church's struggle with its understandings of the faith.

Pressed harder, I would argue that Frances Young brought three fine qualities to her study of the making of the creeds. The first was an understanding of the complexion of history as a form of critical inquiry. As Young herself wrote, 'the fact that we tell the story means that we "create" history, and our own interests and concerns affect the process'. Young was able to bring to life the ways in which generations of Christians, together, struggled with how to understand such ideas as trinity and incarnation, at the same time demonstrating how our reading of their struggles also informs our own interpretation of doctrine. In the wrong hands such hermeneutic questions would be dry bones indeed; but Young revealed their social and ecclesial freshness as never before.

Young's second fine quality was to map a bold theological reading of the development of Christian doctrine onto the story of councils and creeds, bishops and heretics. This reading arguably constitutes the lasting significance of *The Making of the Creeds*, and it is worth taking a few moments just to consider the book's structure.

After a brief introduction and an overview of the period and issues, Young gives the reader five key stages in the development of Christian doctrine: thinking about God and the world; thinking about God and Jesus; thinking about the Holy Spirit and the Church; thinking about the incarnation; and thinking about salvation. I emphasize 'thinking' because the point of this structure is to make people understand how the early Church 'thought' its way through the implications of its belief.

Thus, thinking about God and the world, the 'big picture' of the meaning of creation and its relationship to that which is beyond this world, leads naturally to reflection upon Jesus Christ as the medium by which God and creation are joined. Thinking about Jesus leads to thinking about his authority as Christ, in the power of the Spirit, and the role that power has in establishing the Church. Thinking about the Church, the Body of Christ, makes us think about the incarnate Lord. And thinking about the incarnate Lord should make us think about the question of our own salvation.

What is so brilliant about Young's exposition is the way in which she coaxes the reader to intuit not just the historical inevitability of this process, but also the need to own it theologically. It is not simply a matter of knowing what happened first and what happened next, she seems to be saying. It is far more a matter of realizing the economy of *how* and *why* things happened the way they did, and what that economy means for Christianity. And what this exposition argues for, gently and yet insistently, is the conviction that the development of Christian doctrine *had* to happen the way it did; there was a logic at work, and when you understand it as clearly as possible, then you understand that that logic is the logic of the cross.

The third quality is a consequence of the clarity of Young's exposition, and it is what makes the book so successful as a guide for students. Not only does Young have a certain grasp of the historical facts and a sure understanding of the theological development of the early Church, she also has all the abilities of the born teacher to communicate history and theology in ways that take her readers deeper and deeper into the complexities of the narrative. SCM Press must have realized this, because they equipped the book with a series of charts, tables and glossary that make the development of patristic thought as straightforward as possible. If the time chart is singled out for attention, this is simply because, over two pages, Young manages to itemize every single patristic figure the student is ever likely to encounter – thereby neatly controlling one of the most baffling aspects of the study of this period.

Reading *The Making of the Creeds* again, we can detect something of the liberal élan that made Young a contributor to *The Myth of God Incarnate*, back in the 1970s: an insight into the accessibility and reasonableness of Christian doctrine, well taught and well understood. There is nothing here of the radical or reactionary 1990s, which have brought British theologians to a sharp, caustic appreciation of Christian theology. On the contrary, Young writes with a sense of its practical relevance, and she manages to convey both the intellectual and spiritual joy of knowing about the origin of the creeds.

One of my happiest memories of my time at the University of Birmingham is of Frances Young standing in a pulpit in St James's Cathedral, Chicago, enthralling the congregation with her grasp of the biblical text, its history and its interpretation. That was 1995. I believe that readers of this new edition will have the same experience, and for that SCM Press are to be congratulated and thanked.

Gareth Jones
Professor of Theology
Canterbury Christ Church University College
November 2001

Preface to the first edition

The immediate occasion for writing this brief account was response to an invitation from John Bowden of SCM Press to produce an up-dated version of Alan Richardson's *Creeds in the Making*, an invitation for which I have become the more grateful over the period in which it has been produced. For the genesis of a book is more profound than its immediate stimulus, and the challenge to put pen to paper has crystallized many things that had been long in solution, as well as having a number of side-effects by way of research papers and lectures along the way. To him, and the many students I have taught who have been enthused about the subject, this book is offered in gratitude, and in the hope that there may also be many informal students, particularly those unsure whether they are inside or outside the church, who will find assistance here in understanding what Christianity in its classical form is about.

Maurice Wiles assisted in the latter stages by reading and commenting on the draft, and for this and his long-standing help and encouragement I am grateful: he is, as it were, my academic father. Thanks are also due for practical assistance to Anne Bowen who typed up the three chapters written in my atrocious long-hand during a period of convalescence, and to Elnora Ferguson who produced the index.

November 1990   FRANCES M. YOUNG

Introduction

This account of how classical Christian theology was formed has been put together in response to an invitation to provide a successor to Alan Richardson's *Creeds in the Making*.* It was felt that, valuable though that book remains, scholarship must have moved on since he wrote it in the thirties. It is true that new evidence and new ways of looking at old evidence have modified the story somewhat. Yet the fundamental story and the main characters in it remain much the same. What has changed is the perspective and shape of the book.

Why the very considerable difference in approach? There are a number of major shifts, several of which relate to changes in the wider theological and intellectual scene. The first concerns the understanding of history. The nineteenth century challenged the 'historicity' of the Bible, and in response theological research became obsessed with the 'facts' and theological thinking with the declaration that Christianity is a historical religion. That was Richardson's starting-point, the 'fact' of Jesus and the 'fact' of the resurrection, which were, as he puts it, 'the facts which . . . doctrine was invented to explain' (p. 19). This quotation hints at a second of his concerns, namely the relationship between theology and experience, or to put it another way, between dogma and religion. Primacy was given to the 'experience' of the 'fact' of Jesus and the religious response of faith to it, and the story of credal formation was treated as the process whereby a satisfactory 'second-order' account was reached.

Although these issues have remained concerns at the popular level, the influence of what might be called 'new philosophies' has

* First published 1935, fifteenth impression, SCM Press and Trinity Press International 1990.

dramatically modified the way they would be approached in the light of more recent theological work. We have become aware that to speak of 'facts' apart from interpretation is simply impossible. History is a form of narrative and all narrative constructs involve a process of selection, judgment as to what is significant, discernment of cause and effect, and interpretative patterning. In other words the fact that we tell the story means that we 'create' history, and our own interests and concerns affect the process. This activity of passing on the past is not, however, a purely individualistic matter. It belongs to a community, it is a social construct and is usually related to the formation of identity. There can be no final definitive version of any story, for each generation or interest group 'recon-structs' the story.

Now 'create' does not mean 'invent'. Clearly there are more and less responsible reconstructions, depending on the extent to which disciplined attention has been given to all the available evidence and the investigator has made allowance for presuppositions or prior commitments which might distort the assessment. History is largely 'given': you cannot change the past, nor should you appropriate it in such a way that its 'pastness' is compromised. That is part of what the insistence on 'facts' was about. The change in perspective is simply a recognition that different aspects will present themselves to different investigators, that there can be no absolutely complete or 'neutral' accounts, and that no 'bare event' is accessible to us — indeed even if it were, it would be meaningless.

Nor is 'experience' separable from the process of understanding whereby we make the experience our own. Our experience of the world is itself shaped by the language we use to 'name' things and events, and this language is a social and cultural construct which we learn. This was true for the first Christians too. So their experi-ence of the fact of Jesus and the resurrection involved their response, their interpretative perception: without it they would have experi-enced nothing of significance, still less have been able to communi-cate it. The story of creed formation is not therefore secondary to experience, it is a continuation of the process of forging a new community identity which was inherent in responding to the whole nexus of Jesus-responded-to-and-understood. Theology was involved in the experience, and 'confession' of Jesus cannot be assigned exclusively either to the category of 'religion' or 'dogma'.

This change in perspective is to do with the development of 'hermeneutics', which has been influenced by the 'sociology of knowledge' as well as by linguistic philosophy and structuralism. On the one hand, we live in 'symbolic worlds' which are mediated by our culture and make certain ideas plausible, others implausible, on the other, it is not as simple to distinguish 'literal' meaning from 'myth', 'symbol' or 'metaphor' as used to be thought, nor to state the 'real' non-symbolic meaning of figurative language. This shift is bound to have an increasing effect on the way we assess early Christian thought. It demands that we try to enter their 'world' rather than imagining we can simply remove the superficial dressing of a foreign (indeed primitive) culture and find the real heart of Christian belief, as Richardson's treatment often seems to assume.

We find, then, that history in the sense often assumed in the modern world was not their primary concern, and they would have been baffled by the claim that Christianity is a historical religion. But they were concerned to oppose any suggestion that Jesus was merely a supernatural visitant, an option that was all too plausible in their culture. Such points at which the tendencies of their culture were resisted must surely be highly significant for discerning the distinctive identity of the Christian world-view.

The most significant of these 'anti-culture' developments was probably the Christian doctrine of creation. Over-concentration on christology has obscured the importance of this, for christology itself was shaped by the underlying issues concerning the relationship between God and the world. Creation-doctrine also ensured that despite the temptation to treat resurrection as merely spiritual, its physical character was persistently affirmed, and the sacraments became truly sacramental, the spiritual being mediated through the material creation. In this book, emphasis on these points has dramatically changed the telling of the story, as has attention to a point frequently made in recent scholarship, namely that the doctrinal debates issued from concerns about the reality of salvation, a salvation which, I suggest, was understood in a particular way because it was also affected by the doctrine of creation.

Other changes in perspective are the result of the fact that scholarship has progressed in terms of 'entering their world', partly because of new evidence from new discoveries, like the Dead Sea Scrolls and the Nag Hammadi Library, partly because of the critical process which means the presuppositions of one generation of scholars are challenged by the next and new insights are the result. When Richardson wrote, a distinction between 'Greek' and 'Jewish' culture was axiomatic. We now realize that this was an over-simplification. Even Palestine had been subject to Hellenistic influence for two or three centuries before Christ, and cross-cultural interaction is a very complex business (consider a society like that of India which has been subjected to English and Western influences for a somewhat comparable period). Nor are we so confident we know what 'Judaism' was: for at the very period when Christianity was emerging, 'Judaism' hardly was formed, and there was considerable diversity in 'Jewishness'. Jewish scholars interpreting their own history and traditions have also provided new challenges and contributed new perspectives. We can no longer assert a kind of natural continuity between Christian doctrine and biblical ideas by neatly stripping away the supposed malign influence of Greek philosophy.

When Richardson wrote, it was usual to contrast the 'living God of the Bible' with the abstract philosophical concept of God. We now realize that there were important congruences between the philosophical critique of anthropomorphism and the anti-idolatry of scripture – indeed the namelessness and incomprehensibility of God was a Jewish tradition which would radicalize divine transcendence well beyond what Platonism envisaged: for kinship between the soul and the divine was the basis of Platonic idealism. In other respects, too, perhaps especially in ethical outlook, the reading of the Bible in Greek permitted the recognition of legitimate common ground. So bewailing the 'Hellenization' of Christianity no longer seems appropriate. There was a proper and fruitful marriage of Greek philosophy and Jewish traditions which produced the new thing, Christianity, which defined itself over against both its parents while inheriting many characteristics from each. This book is an attempt to write the story of that process.

I

The Making of the Creeds

Christianity is the only major religion to set such store by creeds and doctrines. Other religions have scriptures, others have their characteristic ways of worship, others have their own peculiar ethics and lifestyle; other religions also have philosophical, intellectual or mystical forms as well as more popular manifestations. But except in response to Christianity, they have not developed creeds, statements of standard belief to which the orthodox are supposed to adhere. Other religions have hymns and prayers, they have festivals, they have popular myths, stories of saints and heroes, they have art forms, and have moulded whole societies and cultures. But they have no 'orthodoxy', a sense of right belief which is doctrinally sound and from which deviation means heresy. In practice, Christianity has all the characteristics mentioned in common with other religions, and like other religions it has taken many different forms and developed many different lifestyles over the centuries as it has been incarnated in different cultures; but in theory Christianity is homogeneous and its homogeneity lies in orthodox belief. Despite the ecumenical movement, Christian groups still claim that their truth is the truth, betraying that this is something they all have in common: namely, a distinction between true belief and false belief. There may in practice be a number of different orthodoxies, but 'orthodoxy' seems characteristic of Christianity.

Now when you stop to think about this, it really is rather surprising. Christianity arose within Judaism: as has so often been said, Judaism is not an orthodoxy, but an orthopraxy – its common core is 'right action' rather than 'right belief' – Judaism was not the source of Christianity's emphasis on orthodoxy, and has formulated its 'beliefs' only in reaction to Christianity. Nor can we find the source in the teaching or attitudes of the founder of this religion: a dispassionate look at the gospel records hardly suggests a figure with episcopal authority propounding dogma and excluding debaters or doubters. So where, then, did this feature of Christianity come from? The purpose of this introductory book is to try and trace how and why Christianity became a credal religion, and how and why doctrine developed as it did. We begin with the creeds themselves: what was the origin and function of the confessions of faith we still find in Christian liturgies – the Apostles' Creed and the Nicene Creed?

There is a legend already developed before the fifth century that prior to setting out to preach the gospel all over the world, the apostles 'first settled an agreed norm for their future preaching so that they might not find themselves, widely separated as they would be, giving out different doctrines to the people they invited to believe in Christ. So they met together in one spot, and, being filled with the Holy Spirit, compiled this brief token, as I have said, of their future preaching, each making the contribution he thought fit; and they decreed that it should be handed out as standard teaching to believers.'* Not much later we find the various clauses each attributed to a named individual apostle! But the Apostles' Creed as we now have it cannot go back to the apostles. For one thing, it is not identical word for word with the creed to which this legend is first attached, though clearly it is a later descendent of what we call 'the Old Roman Creed'. Secondly, neither the Old Roman Creed nor the Apostles' Creed have been used in the Greek Church, which produced its own formulae, similar in style and pattern but not the same in wording. All these different credal formulae, including the Old Roman Creed as well as Eastern forms, emerge around the turn of the third century, and cannot be traced in earlier Christian literature. We must therefore, look for processes of development, for precursors, and we cannot simply accept the legend at face value. In any case, we know that the agreement to adopt universally the creed known as Nicene, was the outcome of decisions by Ecumenical Councils in the fourth century. So clearly there is an historical process to be investigated, by that stage involving political pressures alongside whatever other factors we may identify.

* Rufinus, as quoted in J. N. D. Kelly, *Early Christian Creeds*, Longman, third edition 1972, pp. 1–2.

   In the doctrinal controversy which led to
adoption of the Nicene Creed, we find people
being questioned or challenged offering in rep
faith they received from their bishop, and the
creed-like summaries of doctrine. There is clea
lies behind this is the system of training for baptism and initiation
into the church. From the middle of the fourth century on, we have
a number of series of Lenten lectures surviving from various parts
of the Christian world which give us information about how converts
were prepared for baptism: after three years as 'hearers of the word',
they would be allowed to attend the local bishop's lectures leading
to the rite of initiation which took place on Easter night, so that the
baptizand would die with Christ and rise with him on Easter Sunday
morning. Clearly this practice goes back a century or more at least.
The extant lectures are usually in the form of a commentary on the
creed, so various local creeds can be reconstructed from them; and
during the process, the candidates apparently had to memorize the
creed, so as to recite it back before being accepted and baptized.
Undoubtedly this is the context in which the familiar credal form
was first framed and used. After the adoption of the Nicene Creed,
the local creeds survived, and became Nicene by the insertion of
the particular agreed formulae into each: that seems to be the way
the creed of Constantinople (the one we now use as the 'Nicene'
creed) arose, it then being adopted as the official version at the
Council in 381 because it had a more developed clause about the
Holy Spirit than the formula agreed at the earlier Nicene Council
in 325. Creeds did not originate, then, as 'tests of orthodoxy', but
as summaries of faith taught to new Christians by their local bishop,
summaries that were traditional to each local church and which in
detail varied from place to place. Typical variations can in fact be
observed simply by comparing the two creeds we know from their
continuing usage, for as we have already noted, the 'Nicene' creed
is a local Eastern creed adopted by the Council of Constantinople,
and the 'Apostles'' Creed is a descendent of the Old Roman Creed,
the creed in use in the church at Rome at a comparable date (see
below p. 5).

   Such a comparison reveals a number of interesting points. What
they have in common is the three-part structure, clauses about God

ather, about the Son of God and about the Holy Spirit. Neither them, however, has an explicit doctrine of the Trinity spelled out systematically: the three 'characters' in the story are described and implicitly related to one another, but the word Trinity is not used, and there is no exposition of the doctrine of God as Three-in-One. There is a sense in which the creeds are not themselves a system of doctrine. The variations confirm this observation: the discrete points are perhaps less important than the bearing they have on the whole. It's as though the essential content is indeed a *story*, and as we all know, there are various ways of telling the same story depending on the selection of material, if not the artistry of the narrator. These features are important pointers to the fundamental nature of the creeds: they are summaries of the gospel, digests of the scriptures. As Cyril of Jerusalem put it in his Catechetical Lectures (V.12), 'Since all cannot read the scriptures, some being hindered from knowing them by lack of education, and others by want of leisure, . . . we comprise the whole doctrine of the faith in a few lines.' These were to be committed to memory, treasured and safeguarded, because 'it is not some human compilation, but consists of the most important points collected out of scripture'.

But if the creeds were intended as summaries of scripture, they have an unexpected shape: there is no summary of Israel's history as God's chosen people, no summary of the life and teaching of Jesus, etc. And if there are variations, there are also surprising similarities in detail. The similarities and divergences can be further observed if we add to our two well-known specimens, the creed reconstructed from Cyril's Lectures (and we could add a good many more). In fact, the 'Nicene' creed shares some features of Cyril's creed which are typically Eastern: the concern about the creation of the 'invisible' or spiritual world, as well as 'heaven and earth'; the stress on the pre-existence of Christ as the Word through whom all things were created. It also has one Eastern feature not evident in Cyril's, the provision of an explanation – 'for us men and for our salvation'. Unlike many Eastern creeds, however, including Cyril's, it shares with the Roman creed stress on the Virgin Mary and the Holy Spirit as the means of incarnation. So there are variations but also identical details, and there is a common tri-partite shape. How are all these features to be accounted for?

Table I

The 'Nicene' Creed of 381	The Apostles' Creed	The Jerusalem Creed
We believe in one God, the Father, almighty, maker of heaven and earth, of all things visible and invisible; And in one Lord Jesus Christ, the only-begotten Son of God, begotten from the Father before all ages, light from light, true God from true God, begotten not made, of one substance with the Father, through whom all things came into existence, Who because of us men and because of our salvation came down from heaven, and was incarnate from the Holy Spirit and the Virgin Mary and became man, and was crucified for us under Pontius Pilate, and suffered and was buried, and rose again on the third day according to the Scriptures and ascended to heaven, and sits on the right hand of the Father, and will come again with glory to judge living and dead, of whose kingdom there will be no end; And in the Holy Spirit, the Lord and life-giver, Who proceeds from the Father, Who with the Father and Son is together worshipped and together glorified, Who spoke through the prophets; in one Holy Catholic and apostolic Church. We confess one baptism for the remission of sins; we look forward to the resurrection of the dead and the life of the world to come. Amen.	I believe in God, the Father almighty, creator of heaven and earth; And in Jesus Christ His only Son, our Lord, Who was conceived by the Holy Spirit, born from the Virgin Mary, suffered under Pontius Pilate, was crucified, dead and buried, descended to hell, on the third day rose again from the dead, ascended to heaven, sits at the right hand of God the Father almighty, thence he will come to judge the living and the dead; I believe in the Holy Spirit, the Holy Catholic Church, the communion of saints, the remission of sins, the resurrection of the flesh, and eternal life. Amen.	We believe in one God, the Father almighty, maker of heaven and earth, of all things visible and invisible; And in one Lord Jesus Christ, the only begotten Son of God, Who was begotten from the Father as true God before all ages, through whom all things came into being, Who [was incarnate and] became man, Who was crucified [and buried and] rose again [from the dead] on the third day, and ascended to the heavens, and sat down at the right hand of the Father and will come in glory to judge living and dead, of whose kingdom there will be no end; [And] in one Holy Spirit, the Paraclete, Who spoke in the prophets, and in one baptism of repentance to the remission of sins, and in one Holy Catholic Church, and in the resurrection of the flesh and in life everlasting. Amen.

It seems that the creeds took the form they did in response to the situation in which they arose, that the selection of details related to the challenges presented to the Christian account of things (a point to be fully explored in subsequent chapters), and the common 'catch-phrases' are deeply traditional in oral confessional material pre-dating the formation of the creeds.

The creeds took the form they did in response to the situation in which they arose, namely the context of catechesis and baptism. About half a century earlier than our first evidence of creeds, we find that at the moment of baptism, three questions were customary, to each of which the candidate would reply, 'I believe' (quoted from Ps.-Hippolytus, *Apostolic Tradition*):

Dost thou believe in God, the Father Almighty?

Dost thou believe in Christ Jesus, the Son of God, who was born of the Holy Ghost of the Virgin Mary, and was crucified under Pontius Pilate, and was dead and buried, and rose again the third day, alive from the dead, and ascended into heaven, and sat at the right hand of the Father, and will come to judge the quick and the dead?

Dost thou believe in the Holy Ghost, and the holy church, and the resurrection of the flesh?

After each response and therefore three times in all, the candidate was dipped into the water and submerged. The custom was no doubt based on the dominical command to baptize in the name of the Father, the Son and the Holy Spirit (Matt. 28.19). These questions are sometimes referred to as 'interrogatory creeds', and the more familiar credal forms as 'declaratory creeds'. Exactly what the relationship between the two is, and how the move from one to the other took place, is not clearly documented. The liturgical use of the questions at the moment of baptism survived alongside the development of the creeds and the custom of memorizing a creed and reciting it back before baptism. Whatever the exact relationship, it seems likely that the universal three-part shape of the creed is accounted for by the traditional and well-developed practice of the three questions. It is likely that the detailed content of the three questions showed some of the same local variations, and it is not surprising to find different creeds with the same basic shape emerging as a result of this background.

The common 'catch-phrases' are deeply traditional in oral confessional material pre-dating the creeds, and their selection relates to the challenges presented to the Christian account of things. Already in the early second century, we find 'creed-like' summaries in the works of Ignatius of Antioch:

> For our God Jesus Christ was conceived by Mary according to God's plan, of the seed of David and of the Holy Spirit; who was born and was baptized that by his passion He might cleanse water. (*Ephesians* 18.2)

> Be deaf when everyone speaks to you apart from Jesus Christ, who was of the stock of David, who was from Mary, who was truly born, ate and drank, was truly persecuted under Pontius Pilate, was truly crucified and died in the sight of beings heavenly, earthly and under the earth, who also was truly raised from the dead, His Father raising him . . . (*Trallians* 9)

> . . . being fully persuaded as regards our Lord, that he was truly of David's stock according to the flesh, Son of God by the Divine will and power, begotten truly of the Virgin, baptized by John that he might fulfil all righteousness, truly nailed in the flesh on our behalf under Pontius Pilate and Herod the Tetrarch . . . that through his resurrection He might set up an ensign . . . in one body of His Church . . . (*Smyrnaeans* 1.1–2)

What is noticeable here is the emphasis on the true human birth and true human death of Jesus: undoubtedly the selection and the emphasis were determined by the fact that Ignatius confronted people who were suggesting that Jesus was a kind of human disguise for the truly divine or spiritual Christ, and neither birth nor death were real, a heresy known as 'docetism'. It was such distortions and challenges which affected the selection of certain details. But it is also noticeable that the different creed-like passages exploit certain stereotyped 'catch-phrases', some but not all drawn from scripture, which have clearly been used because they 'ring bells' with people, they are part of the traditional 'in-language' of Christian teaching and worship. At the same time we are not dealing with quotations of a fixed creed, rather with flexible summaries built up as occasion demanded from stereotyped formulae. The other noticeable feature is that these summaries are not Trinitarian in shape, but are clearly precursors of the second clause of the later fixed credal formularies.

Once alert to this kind of material, we can trace it already in the New Testament: from the very beginning, the Christian communities developed a stereotyped in-language to summarize their fundamental teaching or tell their particular story. So Paul seems to 'quote' or adapt traditions and common confessions:

> . . . Christ died for our sins according to the scriptures, and he was buried, and was raised on the third day according to the scriptures, and he appeared to Cephas, then to the Twelve, then to more than five hundred brothers at once . . . then he appeared to James, then to all the apostles . . . (I Cor. 15.3ff.)

> . . . Concerning his Son, who was born of David's seed according to the flesh, who was declared Son of God with power by the Spirit of Holiness when he was raised from the dead, Jesus Christ our Lord, through whom we have received grace . . . (Rom. 1.3ff.)

> Christ Jesus who died, or rather has been raised from the dead, who is on the right hand of God, who also makes intercession for us . . . (Rom. 8.34)

Such passages can be paralleled by many others, not just in the authentic writings of Paul – take, for example, I Peter 3.18ff.:

> For Christ also suffered for sins, the just for the unjust, to bring us to God, slain indeed in the flesh but quickened in the Spirit . . . Who is on the right hand of God, having ascended to heaven, angels, authorities and powers having been subjected to him.

There are good grounds for finding the origin of the set phrases of the creed in such stereotyped confessional language and to see it as deeply traditional, despite the absence of evidence for fixed credal formulae in the early centuries.

From such stereotyped material, selection was made to confront challenges to the 'over-arching story' that enabled Christians to make sense of the world. A couple of generations later than Ignatius we find a number of Christian writers from different parts of the world referring to the *Rule of Faith* or the *Canon of Truth* – Irenaeus in Gaul (modern France), Tertullian in North Africa, Origen in Egypt. This title is given to summaries of the faith which are clearly not fixed – Irenaeus cites it in several different forms, which use different shapes, different selections of details, different stereotyped phrases, but which cover essentially the same ground, and are most typically used to contrast true Christian teaching with the 'knowledge falsely so-called' of the heretics. The particular struggle which provided the context for these will be explored further in the following chapter, but their bearing on the formation of creeds can be observed if their variable and yet consistent texts are carefully pondered (see pp. 10 and 11).

A number of points can be regarded as clear:

1. These people, writing in the late second and early third centuries, did not know a fixed creed in a Trinitarian shape, though they were probably familiar with the use of three questions at baptism in a simpler and less developed form than that quoted above;

2. They were familiar with the use of stereotyped phrases, some scriptural but not all, within the context of summaries of the faith which were not fixed but adaptable to various situations – many of their phrases would appear in creeds, later;

3. They were prepared to refer to such a summary as authoritative in the context of debate with 'false teachers', already referred to as heretics;

4. They regarded such a normative over-view as 'apostolic' and as the standard to which appeal was to be made when controversy about the content or interpretation of scripture arose.

In all these ways, the *Rule of Faith* is clearly an important precursor (or perhaps we should say provides important precursors) to the creeds. Undoubtedly the overall selection made in the *Rule of Faith*, and the use of traditional phrases, profoundly affected the expansion of the second baptismal question, and the development

Table II The Rule of Faith

Irenaeus	Tertullian	Origen (abridged)
For the Church, though dispersed throughout the whole world ... has received from the apostles and their disciples this faith:	Now, as to this rule of faith ... it is, you must know, that which prescribes the belief that	... The holy apostles, when preaching the faith of Christ, took certain doctrines, those namely which they believed to be the necessary ones, and delivered them in the plainest terms to all believers ... The kind of doctrines which are believed in plain terms through the apostolic teaching are as follows:
in one God, the Father Almighty, who made the heaven and the earth and the seas and all things that are in them;	there is one only God, and that he is the Creator of the world, who produced all things out of nothing through his own Word, First of all sent forth;	First, that God is one, who created and set in order all things, and who, when nothing existed, caused the universe to be. He is God from the first creation and foundation of the world, the God of all righteous men (OT heroes listed). This God in these last days, according to the precious announcements made through his prophets, sent the Lord Jesus Christ ....
and in one Christ Jesus, the Son of God, who became incarnate for our salvation;	that this Word is called his Son, and under the name of God, was seen in divers forms by the patriarchs, ever heard in the prophets, at last brought down by the Spirit and Power of God the Father into the Virgin Mary, was made flesh in her womb, and, being born of her, lived as Jesus Christ; thenceforth he preached a new law and a new promise of the kingdom of heaven, worked miracles, was crucified, and rose again the third day;	Then again: Christ Jesus, he who came to earth, was begotten of the Father before every created thing ... in these last times he emptied himself and was made man, was made flesh, although he was God ... He took to himself a body like our body, differing in this alone, that it was born of a virgin and the Holy Spirit. And this Jesus Christ was born and suffered in truth and not in mere appearance, and truly died our common death.

Irenaeus

and in the Holy Spirit, who proclaimed through the prophets the dispensations and the advents, and the birth from a virgin, and the passion, and the resurrection from the dead, and the incarnate ascension into heaven of the beloved Christ Jesus, our Lord, and His future manifestation from heaven in the glory of the Father, to 'sum up all things' (Ephes. 1.10) and to raise up anew all flesh of the whole human race, in order that to Christ Jesus, our Lord and God and Saviour and King, according to the will of the invisible Father, 'every knee should bow, of things in heaven ...' etc. (Phil. 2.10–11). 'and every tongue confess' to him, and that He should execute just judgement towards all; that He may send 'spiritual wickednesses' (Eph. 6.12), and the angels who transgressed and came into a state of rebellion together with the ungodly, and unrighteous, and wicked, and profane among men, into the everlasting fire; but may as an act of grace, confer immortality on the righteous and holy, and those who have kept his commandments, and have persevered in his love, some from the beginning, and others from their repentance, and may surround them with everlasting glory.

Tertullian

He was caught up to the heavens, and sat down at the right hand of the Father;

He sent instead of Himself the power of the Holy Ghost to lead such as believe,

He will come again with glory to take the saints to the enjoyment of everlasting life and of the heavenly promises, and to condemn the wicked to everlasting fire, after the resurrection of both these classes shall have happened, together with the restoration of their flesh.

This rule was taught by Christ, and raises among ourselves no questions except those which heresies introduce ...

Origen

Moreover he truly rose from the dead, and after the resurrection companied with his disciples and was then taken up to heaven.

Then again the apostles delivered this doctrine, that the Holy Spirit is united in honour and dignity with the Father and the Son ...

Next after this the apostles taught that the soul ... will be rewarded according to its deserts after its departure from the world; for it will either obtain an inheritance of eternal life and blessedness ... or it must be given over to eternal fire and torments ... Further there will be a time for the resurrection of the dead ...

(Origen then adds a number of further doctrines as apostolic: freewill, the struggle with the devil, the help of ministering angels in bringing about salvation; and observes a number of doubtful points which are open to investigation.)

Note that a number of abbreviations leave out quotations from scripture.

of a 'declaration' of belief in the catechetical context. It was the welding together of these elements that led to the emergence of creeds as we know them towards the end of the third century.

In tracing this process, we have discerned a number of contributory factors: first, the processes of handing on the faith orally, which already in the New Testament produced stereotyped confessional summaries, and which became much more formalized in '*traditio et redditio*' of the creed, that is, the process of handing it over to be learned by heart and giving it back by recitation; secondly, the need to have a standard summary to which appeal could be made when features of the Christian story were contested; thirdly, the influence of liturgical forms, arising naturally from the close connection between baptism and the teaching-context within which creeds were eventually formulated.

The second of these factors was then to have an over-riding effect on the further development of creeds as 'tests of orthodoxy', but it is important to realize that creeds belonged originally to a different context, and so be able to understand their fundamental character.

As we have already observed, they are not 'Articles of Belief' or a system of doctrine, but rather 'confessions' summarizing the Christian story, or affirmations of the three 'characters' in the story. They tell who God is and what he has done. They invite the convert to make that story and that affirmation his or her own: the word for 'confess' means also 'acknowledge' and even 'praise'. To this extent they are the natural successors to the summary passages of proclamation and acclamation of God and his saving action found in the Jewish scriptures:

Hear, O Israel: the Lord our God, the Lord is one: and you shall love the Lord your God with all your heart, and with all your soul, and with all your might. And these words which I command you this day shall be upon your heart: and you shall teach them diligently to your children, and shall talk of them when you sit in your house, and when you walk by the way, and when you lie down and when you rise . . . (Deut. 5.4)

A wandering Aramean was my father: and he went down into Egypt and sojourned there, few in number: and there he became a nation, great, mighty and populous. And the Egyptians treated us harshly, and afflicted us, and laid upon us hard bondage. Then we cried to the Lord the God of our fathers, and the Lord heard our voice, and saw our affliction, our toil and our oppression: and the Lord brought us out of Egypt with a mighty hand and an outstretched arm, with great terror, with signs and wonders: and he brought us into this place, and gave us this land, a land flowing with milk and honey . . . (Deut. 26.5)

Such affirmations moulded the identity of the Jews, and similarly the creeds (or their precursors) moulded the identity of the new convert. Such Jewish confessions were embedded in worship, and so at first were the Christian confessions that replaced them. Creeds have their genesis in doxology, and they are not to that extent a surprising or uncharacteristic development from Christianity's Jewish background.

But of course they became something else. And the pressures that turned them into 'tests of orthodoxy' were already present, long before imperial and political pressures induced the Ecumenical Councils to use creeds to define acceptable orthodox belief in a search for unity which would inevitably and paradoxically exacerbate division. Already in the New Testament we find internal controversy and attempts to establish true over against false teaching. The conflict with false teaching was deepened in the struggle with Gnosticism in the second century, and with other 'Satanic' heresies as the centuries progressed. (See the next and subsequent chapters.) There can be no doubt that these struggles contributed to the shaping of the creeds, and provided precedents for what happened at Nicaea. Bishops had met in Council before to deal with members of their own number who failed to teach what their consensus demanded. Excommunication had been used before, and false teachers anathematized. The new elements lay in using a creed to define orthodoxy, and in the availability of imperial power to enforce the decisions of the Council and provide the bishops with greater effectiveness in exercising their authority on earth.

So we reach the age of creed-drafting in the fourth century. Few were really happy with the Nicene solution, and when imperial favour tipped towards the anti-Nicenes, Council after Council tried to do a better job. Each competing party had its own creed, and creed after creed was discussed, modified, accepted, only to be superseded by another. After fifty years, this stage came to an end at Constantinople in 381, when the Nicene faith was reaffirmed, though, as we have seen, in the form of a slightly different creed which developed the third article more fully, and therefore answered the needs of a new generation more effectively (see Chapter 4). Seventy years later, when another Council met at Chalcedon to try and settle a rather different controversy, the lesson of this confusing period had clearly been well learned: the Council made no attempt to produce a new creed, reaffirming the creeds of Nicaea and Constantinople, while adding a 'Definition' to explain the right interpretation of the second clause around which controversy had arisen (see Chapter 5).

So controversy undoubtedly contributed to the formation of the creeds, and also to their adaptation as 'tests of orthodoxy'. But the concern with 'true doctrine' or 'orthodoxy' pre-dates its association with creeds, and the authority of bishops to determine true doctrine pre-dates their use of creeds to impose it. In the ancient world the church was unique in imposing this kind of exclusivity, and exploring the creeds has not yet resolved the question why, though clearly the issue of Christian *identity* is important. As we explore the history of doctrinal development we may find more indication of the fundamental factors affecting this. Provisionally we may note the following possibilities:

1. That 'truth' became an issue very rapidly because the Christian story was adapted and exploited by groups with very different views of how to account for 'reality' – after all, the New Testament itself bears witness to deep internal conflicts, not just about practice, but also about belief;

2. That 'truth' became a priority because Christianity inherited the exclusive loyalty of Judaism to the one true God, and could not allow that other revelations, or other gods, had any reality – both 'paganism' and 'philosophy' allowed the possibility of many different ways to truth, and a multiplication of revelations of the gods, so the Christian revelation could easily have been assimilated to this syncretistic amalgam if it had not inherited Jewish opposition to idolatry and religious exclusiveness;

3. That the experience of rejection and persecution from both Jews and pagans, an experience which led Christians to claim they were a 'third race', forged the earliest Christian groups into close-knit, highly disciplined groups, prepared to accept their leaders as the authoritative bearers of the tradition which had laid its exclusive claim upon all the group's members, given them a new identity and exposed them to persistent ridicule if not danger.

All these factors stimulated cohesion and need for authority, and this focussed both on practice – ethics and lifestyle – and on belief. But they also sowed seeds of conflict or provoked splinter-groups. All this will become painfully apparent as our story unfolds. So we are left with a question best left open for the present: was there something about the nature of Christian claims in themselves that made Christianity search for 'orthodoxy', and so gave it a distinctive, and in many ways disturbing, characteristic? For the idea of 'ortho-doxy' cannot but breed intolerance. But the results are not merely negative: concern about truth, about the ways things really are, was also the fruit of this distinctive feature – and that surely is a driving force indispensable to human development. Perhaps it is no accident that science was conceived in the womb of a Christian civilization.

2

One God, Creator of Heaven and Earth

As Christianity triumphed and set about the suppression of paganism, nature was 'de-mystified'. For centuries, sacred groves of trees,
mysterious natural beauty-spots, caves and springs had been
religious sites, where the gods and spirits of nature were treated
with respect. Christian fanatics fearlessly cut down trees in the battle
against idolatry. Nature was not to be worshipped, but rather the
one true God, nature's Creator. If this laid the creation open to
destruction and exploitation, it also eventually gave it the 'autonomy'
necessary for scientific investigation to be possible.

But the doctrines enshrined in the first clause of the creeds were
hard won. At first sight, this may seem surprising. After all, were
they not inherited from Judaism? The answer is 'yes' and 'no'. The
development of the specific theory that the world was created 'out
of nothing' by the one true God who truly is the Creator, belongs
to the early Christian centuries, and arose largely out of a debate
internal to the church, though it was conducted against the background of the wide spectrum of theories or beliefs about the origins
of the universe which existed in the ancient world.

For us, monotheism and the idea of God as the First Cause are so
closely identified with a religious view of life as a result of centuries of
Christian dominance that it is hard to think back to a time when it
was not obvious but contentious *within* religious thinking. The context in which Christianity was born and came to maturity was
incurably polytheistic, and those philosophies which speculated
about a divine first cause, did so by analogy with human creativity,
suggesting a 'matter' or 'substratum' with which the Creator worked.
Christianity started with Jewish assumptions, with an exclusive
loyalty to the one true God of the Jewish scriptures who was
acclaimed as Creator, but this did not exclude the existence of other

supernatural beings, whether angels or demons, and the story of creation in Genesis seemed to presuppose 'something' out of which God created, bringing order to chaos. Within Judaism, circles affected by apocalyptic tended to view the world as presently under the dominion of God's adversary, Satan, who is the 'ruler of this world' even according to John's gospel. The unity and sovereignty of God were not quite as clear-cut as we might imagine, and it was in this area that the first bitter internal struggle was focussed, the struggle with Gnosticism.

The Christian bishops and thinkers who took up the pen to oppose Gnostic forms of Christianity, give the impression that it was a Christian heresy, a deviant form of Christian belief inspired by the devil and corrupting its original purity. The evidence they provided about their opponents, however, suggested that external influences had been profoundly significant. The great scholar, Harnack, referred to Gnosticism as 'the radical Hellenization of Christianity',* and many considered Greek philosophy an important factor in its development. Then others observed that some of its features were better accounted for by influences from the Persian East, from Zoroastrianism, and that it seemed to be a much bigger phenomenon than a mere Christian heresy. New discoveries fuelled the scholarly enthusiasm for viewing Gnosticism as pre-Christian, indeed as an important stimulant to the development of Christianity itself: for it now appeared to be a widespread religious tendency reflecting the syncretism and pessimism of the Hellenistic age. Then people began to pick up clues that suggested a specifically Jewish matrix for Gnosticism, and for linking it with apocalyptic. Although contested in some quarters, the present scholarly consensus generally regards Gnosticism as a serious threat to Christianity already in New Testament times, and as more than a Christian heresy. The discovery of original Gnostic texts has made this a favourite area for research, and it is not altogether clear what conclusions will eventually establish themselves. The following are still contentious questions: How exactly are we to define Gnosticism, and so enable meaningful distinctions to be made? At what date is it possible to say that

* Adolf von Harnack, *History of Dogma*, English translation 1894, Vol. I, p. 226.

Gnosticism really existed as a serious option? Can it be regarded as a movement sufficiently coherent to provide opposition to Paul? Or to influence the theology of John's gospel? Where are we to look for its origins? Happily most of these questions can be left open, and we can still glean enough for our purposes in this chapter.

The fundamental difficulty lying behind all these questions is that in modern scholarship the term 'Gnosticism' has come to cover a wide variety of things: To the Church Fathers, the problems seemed a bit more focussed because they faced a number of distinct but similar sects and groupings, often called after their 'founders' and linked in the mind of their orthodox opponents as the 'knowledge (*gnōsis*) falsely so-called' mentioned in I Tim. 6.20, such groups as the Valentinians, the Naassenes, the Marcosians, Simonians, Sethians and Barbelognostics. Some of the common features of these groups can certainly be linked with a wider set of attitudes found in other ancient literature, notably the so-called Hermetic literature, revelatory material attributed to Hermes, the traditional messenger of the gods. These common attitudes include a profound pessimism about this life coupled with promises of a spiritual world associated with divine light, life and knowledge. Undoubtedly this tendency to regard the body as a tomb (*sōma-sēma* was the Greek jingle) and the desire for escape through 'higher knowledge' was very common, and could claim a sophisticated, philosophical pedigree on the basis of some of Plato's thought. It is significant, however, that the Neoplatonist Plotinus was as deeply opposed to Gnostics as Christian bishops. We need to look for what distinguishes Gnosticism from the general attitudes to understand this opposition, while recognizing that Gnostics could use language that appeared perfectly acceptable to the unwary. The *Gospel of Truth* has a spirituality which makes it good devotional reading in the tradition of the Johannine material, unless you are alerted to the Valentinian teaching implied by it. It took the church in Rome a while to recognize that Valentinus was not an acceptable member. Gnostic groups functioned *inside* the church and on its fringes, and it was subtly attractive. That was what made it so subversive, and that was what led to the efforts to suppress it. For some researchers, Elaine Pagels, for example, this process has seemed the great betrayal, the suppression of free-thinking and feminism by totalitarian bishops.* But such a judgment fails to grasp the insidious nature of the Gnostic alternative and the tenuous position of bishops in the days of the determinative struggle. The outcome of the struggle, however, certainly contributed to the identity of Christianity as a dogmatic religion, and to the development of authority structures in the Christian organization.

Whether or not the struggle began as early as Paul's lifetime the first to clarify the fundamental issues was Irenaeus, bishop of Lyons at the end of the second century. The different groups he criticizes certainly had different emphases, different accounts of the origins of things and different positions in detail. But the common features were (1) a distinction between the Creator God (the Demiurge) and the ultimate Father; (2) an account of the origin of all things which involved a pre-cosmic 'fall', so treating the material universe as the result of an accident or of sin; (3) an estimate of human nature which offered re-union with the divine for the spiritual élite, who were sparks trapped in the material universe, and who would be released by the secret 'knowledge' purveyed by the esoteric group, but dismissed the 'material' as beyond redemption, and regarded ordinary church members as second class. Such views were diametrically opposed to the essentials inherited from Judaism, loyalty to the one true God who created the universe and said it was good; for they involved a fragmentation of the divine nature and a devaluation of creation. It is no surprise in the light of this, to find that the first clause of the Rule of Faith and then of the creeds struck the note that it did. Yet paradoxically these very features of Gnosticism suggest that the movement did arise within Judaeo-Christian circles: for they represent an alienation from belief in One Supreme Creator, and only Jewish tradition had such a belief. We can also see how contemporary apocalyptic ideas about the world being under the dominion of the devil could flip over into the view that the devil was the Creator, the 'god of this world'. It has been suggested that the catalyst for this pessimistic view was disappointment in Jewish circles when the revolts against Rome failed to bring about the Messianic kingdom: hopes were then projected on to the heavens, and despair about this world set in. Prophecy lost its meaning and salvation became escape.

* See Elaine Pagels, *The Gnostic Gospels*, Penguin 1982.

This approach to explaining Gnosticism is encouraged by the interesting links between apocalyptic symbolism and the highly symbolic and allegorical language of gnostic texts, by the common imagery and number symbolism, by similar motifs such as heavenly journeys and revelations, by common themes such as the contrast between light and darkness, life and death. While many of the newly-discovered Gnostic texts appear non-Jewish, exploiting Eastern religious or pagan motifs, astrology and magic, many others reveal how a number of these sects reinterpreted Genesis. As usual in the various accounts details differ, but the general principles are similar: the 'jealous God' of Genesis, the Demiurge who created the universe, is an inferior being, 'jealous' of the spiritual world he is barely aware of; the serpent is the 'goody' in the story, the embodiment of the spiritual principle of wisdom, who brings to humanity knowledge of good and evil, so enabling the divine spark in Adam to reach self-knowledge and escape from the clutches of the Demiurge. Sethian Gnostics saw the primaeval figure of Seth as the 'saviour' spirit who is from time to time revealed, and appeared in Jesus Christ. Many Gnostics saw Christ as the supernatural Redeemer who brought redemption from the flesh and the material universe by revelation of the spiritual world and of the Gnostic's true origin and nature. So Gnostics had their plausible ways of reading scripture, and they had a gospel of salvation. Many thought they had the truth.

But the logic of their position involved a very selective reading of scripture, and a reading which ran counter to the traditions inherited by the church. To begin with, Jesus Christ became a sham, his incarnation was not real, his passion could not have happened. 'Jesus' was simply the human disguise worn by the supernatural Christ whose principal function was to reveal the spiritual world, which he did to certain select disciples after the resurrection. Some suggested that Simon of Cyrene died on the cross, for 'Jesus' disappeared before the passion; others spoke of the spiritual Christ departing from the flesh before the passion. Clearly Ignatius at the beginning of the second century faced docetic views of this kind (see above p. 7). Naturally the resurrection on such views was not *physical*; the flesh, the body, was irrelevant, indeed despicable as part of the fallen material universe. Irenaeus was able to add that believers of this kind could not really participate in the sacraments: for the eucharist takes the material things of life, and affirms their goodness by offering them in thanksgiving. It could not be reduced to mere symbolism, which is what Gnostics loved. So, the consequences of these attractive spiritual teachings being unacceptable, their basic tenets must be invalid.

How then were such views to be met? First, Irenaeus was able to indulge in a certain amount of ridicule. Much Gnostic teaching, and this has been confirmed by some of the Gnostic texts now rediscovered, concerned itself with elaborate accounts of the precosmic process which produced the present unsatisfactory situation. Some of the ideas incorporated in these accounts were interesting and sophisticated, but they were easily represented as absurd myths and genealogical speculations. This Irenaeus contrived to do with the Valentinian account, which we can take as a typical example. The ultimate Forefather was a great Bythos, an abyss, infinite and incomprehensible. There emerged alongside him Thought, known also as Grace, and Silence. He took her as consort and deposited a seed in her; and the pair produced Mind, known also as the Only-Begotten, and Truth, another male-female pair. From these came Word and Life, Design and Wisdom (Sophia), and the eight primal Aeons constituted the Ogdoad. The original Ogdoad gave rise to further Aeons who made up the Decad and the Dodecad, a total of thirty Aeons constituting the spiritual world, the *plēroma* (fullness). One key question in contemporary philosophy was how the Many related to the ultimate One, how the One ground of all Being could produce the complexity of many things. The Gnostic scheme was one kind of answer, the spiritual world having been produced by a process of emanation from the ultimate divine infinite – indeed many of the names of the Aeons reflected philosophical interests. But philosophical sophistication was married with implied sexual imagery of a mythological kind, each pair of apparent abstracts consisting of a masculine and a feminine word. How far away are the gods and goddesses of traditional religion? In the *Book of Baruch*, summarized by Hippolytus, another anti-gnostic writer, a parallel Gnostic scheme appears in the dress of Jewish angels, whose names in any case often expressed attributes of the divine: Gabriel = Might of God, Phanuel = Face of God, Michael = Who is like God?,

Raphael = God heals. The spiritual world of Gnostic revelation in this guise seems not unrelated to the heavenly court of Jewish apocalyptic, though cosmological interests and philosophical concerns have given it a new and disturbing slant. For Irenaeus the threat to the unity of God was real: this fragmentation of the divine undermined loyalty to the one true God, and on his side, he was not afraid to adopt philosophy to show how crude and inadequate the Valentinian account was. The one God contains all things, while being uncontainable, and therefore is infinite and indivisible. Gnostic fragmentation of the divine would not do. The being of God's self was not the stuff out of which further beings were produced, least of all by quasi-sexual activity.

Having shown how the spiritual world is 'furnished', the Valentinian myth went on to explain the material world. Sophia (wisdom) was overtaken by passion, wanting to 'know' the ultimate Forefather. In principle it was impossible to know one who was infinite and therefore incomprehensible, so her rash attempt led to an 'abortion', a misconceived creature Achamoth (a corruption of the Hebrew word for wisdom). The word 'know' has a *double entendre*, as the sexual imagery becomes both explicit and symbolic: F. C. Burkitt suggested that the myth was a way of suggesting the sin and folly of human philosophy attempting to understand everything, and failing.* Sophia committed the primal act of *hybris*, that overreaching human pride which always leads to tragic disaster (*nemesis*). Achamoth was expelled from the pleroma, and produced the Demiurge, who being ignorant of the spiritual world, created the material universe. Sophia wanted to save her offspring which got fragmented and mixed up in this alien environment.

Ridicule was no longer enough, for God the Creator was reduced to an ignorant and incompetent being, and the unity of God's creating and redeeming activity was completely undermined. The unity of the scriptures was destroyed, and the sense of God's purposes, predicted in prophecy and providentially worked out in Christ, was completely lost. How was this challenge to be met?

Irenaeus had two basic approaches, both of which were of profound significance for the future of Christian doctrine. On the one

---

* F. C. Burkitt, *Church and Gnosis*, Cambridge University Press 1932.

hand, he created the first 'systematic theology', a comprehensive attempt to see Christian teaching as a coherent whole. Using scripture and some ideas pioneered by his predecessors, he developed the theory of *recapitulation*. The Gnostics were fascinated by Genesis, so he took Genesis and showed what it was really about. The one true God, who created the universe and all things in it, set Adam in Paradise as the crown of his creation. But Adam was innocent, like a child, and misused the freedom God had given him: he was disobedient. As a result God's good creation was corrupted, though still fundamentally good. Christ came as the new Adam. He was fully human, and as a human being he went over the same ground as Adam did, reversing the process, succeeding where Adam failed. So the redemption of the whole of creation was begun, and would eventually be consummated. Thus the eucharistic bread and wine, material things, could become the vehicle of spiritual things, for matter was *not* inherently evil, a mistake, a prison. The body itself would be raised to new life within a new creation. Salvation was not escape from this created order, but rather a re-creation of what was fundamentally good, but gone wrong. This was the way to understand the whole story, because then the activity of the prophets, and the whole story of God's dealings with humanity could make coherent sense. Belief in one God, who is the Creator God, was vindicated, though Irenaeus did not take the next logical step of challenging the view that the world's corruption was in part due to the temptation of Satan, who remained God's adversary, though in principle overcome and destined for final defeat.

Irenaeus' second approach was to appeal to the authority of tradition. It was not so easy or as straightforward as we might think to appeal to scripture. The church had, as yet, no clearly defined Bible. Certain scriptures had been inherited from the Jews: the Law and the Prophets, and some Writings, like the Psalms, the collections of Wisdom attributed to Solomon, and some apocalypses. Apart from the Law and the Prophets, there were no clearly determined rules about which so-called scriptures were to be regarded as authoritative. Besides the Jewish writings, there were various Christian books in circulation, but it was not always clear which of these carried authority: how many of the gospels could be regarded as reliable and safe? Were the epistles of Paul acceptable? What about all the other epistles floating about? Some, like the heretic Marcion, had tried to establish a limited 'canon' or rule about acceptable books. Marcion thought the Jewish scriptures should be abandoned, since they referred to a wrathful Deity who could not be the same as the God of Love revealed by Jesus, and after all Paul said that in Christ the Law had an end: Paul's epistles and an expurgated version of Luke's gospel alone contained the truth. Others, like Valentinus, produced their own gospel; others again circulated gospels attributed to apostles like Thomas or Philip but of dubious origin. To these people, the prophets meant little or nothing, though some, as we have seen, appealed to a twisted interpretation of Genesis, and were prepared to accept the Law provided it was interpreted in a radically spiritual and symbolic way through allegory. Clearly the Bible could not constitute an arbiter or court of appeal when its content and interpretation were matters of dispute.

Irenaeus did appeal to the Bible, however, and he did so by carefully discerning the consensus of tradition about which books were authoritative and how they were to be interpreted. This tradition he traced back to the apostles. He lists the bishops of Rome to show the continuity of tradition from Peter. He speaks of his own youthful connection with Polycarp in Asia Minor (modern Turkey), and Polycarp knew the apostles. This solid tradition gave Irenaeus assurance that certain books were authoritative, and that their unified message was lodged in what he referred to as the *Rule of Faith* or the *Canon of Truth* (see above pp. 9ff.). Identically the same God is referred to in the inherited Jewish scriptures and the more recent Christian writings: Irenaeus himself may not have meant to refer to these collections of books when he used the phrases Old Testament (= covenant) and New Testament, but very soon the connection would be made. That same one God was Creator, and he had providential purposes set out in the prophets. This world and the course of events played out in its history is to be understood as belonging to this one God, whose redeeming work was accomplished in Jesus Christ and will be eventually consummated when the End comes. The discrete books of what we know as a single Bible were given their unity by reference to a traditional summary of the over-arching story they told; only in the light of this authoritative tradition were they to be interpreted.

So it was that the struggle with Gnosticism focussed the mind of the church on the question of truth, and its organization on the issue of authority. There are places in the New Testament where it seems a bit unclear whether this is God's world or not: it is the 'ruler of this world' that Jesus overcomes in John's gospel, and believers are to be 'in the world' but not 'of the world'. Paul's language is open to interpretation in terms of a dualism between the 'flesh' and the 'spirit', and both the Pauline and Johannine Christ could appear to be a divine figure visiting a world to which he did not belong – except that for both the passion is real. When the Gnostics really forced the issue, the question was clear: Is this God's world or not? It was a question about the truth, about the way things are. There could be no compromise between truth and falsehood. But how was truth to be maintained? Already in the New Testament there is concern about false teaching. Paul's epistles reveal conflicts of authority, and later epistles seek authorities to guarantee the true teaching, often appealing to the apostles. Increasingly in the second century the *episcopos* (superintendent or overseer) was seen as the bearer of the apostolic tradition, and therefore the doctrinal authority, though prophets and martyrs had a charisma that could challenge this. The insidious esoteric groups with their claims to 'secret knowledge' passed down from apostles who had received private revelations, and their élitist scorn and criticism of the naive views of their fellow church members, reinforced the need for authority, and for exclusion of incompatible views. This early struggle within the church bears the weight of responsibility for the 'credal' nature of Christianity.

But it also explains much of the selection of details that became traditional in the creeds: insistence on the one God who is Creator; insistence on the genuine human birth and death of Jesus Christ (rather than a summary of his teaching); focus on the prophetic Spirit who pointed to the overall purposes of God and inspires their accomplishment. The factuality of all this within this world, a world which belongs to God since he is its Creator, became crucial. It was once thought that what makes Christianity itself is the fact that it is a 'historical faith', that it takes history seriously. There is a measure of truth in this, though it seems doubtful whether the early church was concerned about history in quite the way we are. It *was* concerned, however, with the reality of this world as the stage on which God worked out his purposes, this world as the world God created, has redeemed and will re-create.

Precisely how the doctrine emerged that the creation was 'out of nothing' is not altogether clear, but this too seems to be, directly or indirectly, the result of the struggle with Gnosticism. It is first clearly enunciated as a positive doctrine a bit before the time of Irenaeus by Theophilus of Antioch. Not that we cannot find linguistic precedents for such a statement, but the problem is to decide what the implications of the earlier examples may be. Prior to this period the doctrine was certainly not taken for granted. In the mid-second century the apologist Justin Martyr clearly believed that God had created the universe out of pre-existent 'matter'.

The Apologists were a group of writers who sought to explain the Christian faith to the wider world of Graeco-Roman civilization, often addressing their works to the Emperor, though that may be a literary fiction. This wider context of the somewhat parochial struggle with Gnosticism is often forgotten: Christians were a powerless minority subject to persecution, and much maligned and misunderstood – a dangerous superstition. Justin was well-acquainted with the views of sophisticated people – indeed, he saw himself as a philosopher. But he had come to believe that Christianity was the true philosophy, a belief for which he eventually paid with his life. He gives no hint of the internal battle with Gnosticism: his attention is on the far more weighty questions posed by philosophy, pagan religion and the Jews, who did not after all recognize Jesus as the Messiah, the fulfilment of their prophecies.

Justin inherited the Greek enquiry into the origin of things which had shifted speculation from mythological story-telling to philosophical theory. Most sophisticated Greeks thought in terms of the universe, or its fundamental constituents at any rate, being eternal. What needed explanation was why things are as they are, how they got ordered, rather than how they got created. Thus Stoics spoke of the fundamental material of the universe, its *archē* or first principle, as being fire, which they thought of as the most discrete kind of matter, and as a sort of spiritual divine substance, the Logos (= Word, Reason, Order), permeating all things, and giving them order. Periodically, they believed everything returns to the cosmic fire, and then is, as it were, distilled out of it again in great cycles, the whole process eternally taking place under divine providence. Epicureans believed everything to be composed of atoms: what exists is purely a matter of chance, and the stream of atoms is without beginning or end. Atoms collide and cohere for a while, but will then break up. So death is simply disintegration, and need not be feared. There must be gods, because people see visions of them, but there's no need to worry about them either: they too are beings composed of atoms who happen to live a perfect, happy life elsewhere – they don't care about us, so why should we care about them. The Epicureans, like the Christians, were accused of being atheists. Their ideas were little regarded, but illustrate the universal acceptance of a kind of 'steady state' view: the basic constituents were simply eternal and had no beginning. Plato is more significant, but he too attributed no beginning to things: he had explained the world, at any rate in the *Timaeus*, as being the outcome of an eternal mind, the Demiurge, ordering eternal matter according to eternal and immaterial forms or ideas, and it was this which caught the imagination of Platonists in Justin's day rather than some of his other attempts to understand how things are. The ultimate One of the *Parmenides* and Good of the *Republic* tended to be conflated with the divine Mind and turned into a sort of Creator God. So Jewish and early Christian writers found Plato congenial, and suggested he had got his ideas from Moses. Plato's term 'Demiurge' became the standard way of referring to the Creator. But the natural view was that just as Plato's Demiurge ordered pre-existing matter, so too did the Creator God of Genesis: for the earth was formless and void. The waters of chaos became the 'receptacle' of God's creative ordering of things according to the eternal Ideas or Forms which existed in his Mind. Coupled with other ideas about a World-soul, interpreted along Stoic lines as the divine Spirit or Logos (= Word) permeating all things, a sophisticated view of God as transcendent and immanent, and as providentially ordering all things emerged in the philosophy of the Alexandrian Jew, Philo, and it was this kind of conception that Justin Martyr naturally adopted.

A couple of new directions emerge in Justin. The Creator God, the matter he used, and the Ideas by which the matter was ordered, may all have been eternal, but creation is no longer 'timeless'. Taking

Genesis literally, and treating Plato's myth in the *Timaeus* literally also, Justin speaks of a beginning, of an act of creation. He also identifies the Logos, or immanent aspect of God, as a kind of mediating being, the instrument through whom the transcendent God created, then permeates, orders, reveals, and inspires, and through whom he redeemed – for it is this pre-existent Word of God who became incarnate in Jesus. This development will need further discussion in later chapters. The point here is that Justin breaks with philosophical tradition by positing a specific act of creation, a beginning, rather than an eternal process, but he does not suggest that that creative act produced the world 'out of nothing'. Was this simply too novel?

Novelty would not seem to be the problem: the idea had been canvassed before in philosophical circles. But it had always been dismissed on the grounds that if things were created 'out of nothing' they would seem to be a sham, unreal, insubstantial. For someone like Justin, the implications were therefore quite unacceptable, and they would seem to be so for all Christians opposed to Gnostic docetism. The world could not be dismissed as unreal anymore than it could be designated as inherently evil. How then could Irenaeus adopt the idea?

Tertullian, the North African Christian who like Irenaeus struggled against Gnostic heretics as well as many others, perhaps gives us the clue. Arguing with a Platonist Christian, he denied both that God created out of himself, and that he created out of eternal matter (*Against Hermogenes*). What was left? He must have created out of nothing. Why the need to deny the other options? The need was surely created by the struggle with Gnosticism. The eternal matter of Platonism was a somewhat recalcitrant medium, and for Gnosticism matter had become the prime enemy. Matter tended to become a second principle alongside God, even opposed to God. This dualism was now seen to be undermining the affirmation of the one true God who was the sole *archē*, the beginning, the origin of all things. Irenaeus, in developing his concept of God, had begun to claim his boundlessness, as the being who contains all things without being contained, as unlimited in his power and goodness. To suggest God's infinity was a natural development of the claim to the total sovereignty of the one true God, though foreign to the

Greek philosophical tradition which distrusted 'infinity' as lacking form or definition, and tended to ascribe it to the chaos of unformed matter. The developing stress on the unity and infinite transcendence of God left no room for an eternal matter limiting his being or his creativity. So God could not have created out of eternal matter. Nor could he have created out of himself. We have already seen Irenaeus' resistance to the fragmentation of the divine so characteristic of Gnosticism. Emanation of created things from the divine source of all being became associated with such Gnostic schemata, and totally unacceptable. Furthermore, it suggested a process of nature or necessity to which the divine being was subject. So what alternative was there but creation out of nothing? And was not *this* the best way of affirming the power and greatness of God over against the creatureliness of all other beings?

The significance of 'out of nothing' primarily lies in what it says about God. The suggestion that God created out of nothing first appears in Jewish texts of the Hellenistic period, either glorifying the Creator: 'Thou callest into life by thy Word that which is not' (II Baruch 48.8), or encouraging martyrs to trust in a God of such power: 'Look at heaven and earth and see everything that is in them, and recognize that God did not make them out of things that existed.' (II Maccabees 7.28). Did such texts mean to imply that the world was a sham, as philosophers assumed? The suspicion that apocalyptic literature and early martyr-literature might imply a certain unreality about the world so as to encourage disregard of death, hardly does justice to the focus of these texts, which is clearly the unique power of the Creator God. The early prophetic writing of the Christian Hermas says that 'First of all you have to believe that there is one God, who has founded and organized the universe, and has brought the universe out of nothing into existence.' Such affirmations are surely a natural development of the biblical insistence upon the mighty difference between God the Creator and all his creatures: 'my ways are not your ways, nor are my thoughts your thoughts' (Isaiah 55.8). Eventually this tradition would lead to quite explicit denials of the view that human souls were eternal or in some sense divine, to the insistence upon the essential contingency of all God's creatures; for God alone is self-existent, and the creation was an act of his will, not arising from nature or necessity. Meanwhile, the verbal precedents noted enabled Irenaeus and his contemporaries to adopt the theory of creation out of nothing in a positive way, and use it unashamedly in a context in which the philosophical question of origins had become important. In view of his total argument, he could never be accused of implying that the world, being created out of nothing, was a sham or lacked reality: for the whole burden of his work was a defense of the material creation as the good work of a good creator.

So philosophical development of the theory that God created out of nothing was stimulated, it seems, by argument with the Gnostics, but it came to distinguish Christianity from all other philosophies in the ancient world. It is one example of many where Christians did not in the end adopt the cultural norms of their society, but stood out against them. Yet it was the pressures of that culture which drove them to explore the questions in the way they did, and Justin shows how the outcome might have been different. Nevertheless, from the time of Irenaeus and Tertullian, the doctrine of creation out of nothing was firmly established, and specifically argued against competing philosophical theories. It also had important further development within Christian theological thinking, especially in the ideas of Athanasius of Alexandria, the crucial fourth-century theologian (see Chapters 3 and 4).

For Athanasius, creation out of nothing accounted for the human predicament. God had chosen to endow the human race with his 'image', with the life and reason of the divine Logos himself. But disobedience to God's commandment meant loss of the Logos. As a result humanity was drifting back to nothingness from which it had been called into being: loss of the Reason of the Logos meant ignorance, evident in idolatry and immorality, loss of the life of the Logos spelt death. So humanity was on the way to annihilation, and already showed signs of corruption. Mortality was the awful consequence of sin. From this predicament, Jesus Christ came to save humankind, and this was effected by re-endowing human nature with the Logos through the incarnation. The incarnation was thus an act of re-creation. Particular human beings were mortal by their participation in Adam, but could become immortal by participation in Christ, by being adopted as 'sons' of God through being incorporated into the Son of God, the new humanity, the Logos-endowed humanity. 'He became human (man) that we might become divine (god)', affirmed Athanasius (*De Incarnatione* 54), echoing Irenaeus' statement that 'he became what we are that we might become what he is' (*Adversus Haereses* V. praef.). The creativity of God became the key theological concept by which salvation was understood, and the radical nature of that creativity was clarified by the doctrine, now irrevocably established, that God's original act of creation brought things into being out of nothing.

This doctrine also reinforced the Christian insistence that it was not the creation that should be worshipped and admired, but creation's Creator. So a Christian preacher like Basil of Caesarea, one of the great fourth-century Fathers known as the Cappadocians, could produce a series of sermons on the opening chapters of Genesis which both opposed all philosophical theories about the universe while exploiting the knowledge and wisdom about the natural world assembled by ancient 'scientists' like Aristotle to celebrate the wonders of creation and enhance the glory of God. Similarly, his brother Gregory of Nyssa, and other Christian writers like Nemesius of Emesa could embrace the anatomical theories of Galen, and accept without question contemporary understanding of human nature as a composite of body and soul, exploring ideas about the interplay of the two in sense perception and emotion, while setting the whole in a new perspective, through the radical understanding of humanity as creaturely, and as created for God's glory. Philosophical interest in ethics and in divine providence also found itself transferred into a new dimension through Christian insistence on the creative purposes of the one God who chose to create and whose will is expressed in his creative activity. Another great Cappadocian, friend of Basil and his brother, Gregory of Nazianzus, would spell out what they all understood: that God's essence was incomprehensible, but his existence and his attributes could be known through his works. The Creator was partially revealed in his creation; so contemplation of creation became one mode of spirituality, alongside the negative route of denying that God was anything like anything else.

The negative route, the insistence that God was invisible, intangible, incorporeal, unchangeable, indivisible, impassible, infinite and incomprehensible, that he was not part of the creation, but utterly 'other', the source of all creatures, not one of them – that way of reaching a conception of God had over-riding importance, not least because it undermined the polytheism, idolatry and crude anthropomorphism of popular religion and mythology, the paganism which was a kind of nature worship and surrounded the early Christian communities on all sides. However, if the doctrine of creation could lead to a proper evaluation of it as the good work of a good Creator, it could also lead to a de-valuing of it as it was de-mystified. And so as Christianity triumphed, fanatical monks began their destructive tree-chopping in their vicious campaigns against idolatry, and the ascetic movement exacerbated the tendency to de-value the good things of life, the pleasures of the body, sex and beauty. Christian history suggests that in some ways the world-denying tendencies of Gnosticism were never entirely eliminated. Spirit and flesh have continued to contend with one another. Yet the doctrines won in the struggle against Gnosticism were never entirely overlaid. Extreme asceticism was anathematized, and a committed ascetic like the great preacher, John Chrysostom, preached the goodness of marriage, and the equal validity of living the Christian life in the wilderness and in the city: holiness and perfection were moral ideas for all, whatever the circumstances. The balance has never perhaps been successfully maintained, yet the principle is enshrined in the first clause of the creed: we believe in one God, Creator of heaven and earth. So the creation is not to be worshipped, yet it is good and it does reveal something of its Maker. So it is to be regarded with wonder and thanksgiving. Such an attitude not only fosters an appropriate spirituality, but also inspired the beginnings of empirical research, work like that of the eighteenth-century clergyman, Gilbert White, the author of *The Natural History of Selborne* who first engaged in field work, practised precise observation and pioneered behavioural science. Without the elimination of Gnosticism, Christianity would have become a mystical escapism, and would have fragmented into disparate sects of a truly 'other-worldly' and irrelevant character. There would have been no Christendom, no Christian civilization. Self-definition in terms of beliefs about reality, about truth, was unavoidable in view of the Gnostic challenge, and it was this that committed Christian believers to this world and not just the next.

3

One God and One Lord Jesus Christ

> If these men worshipped no other God but one, perhaps they
> would have a valid argument against the others. But in fact they
> worship to an extravagant degree this man who appeared recently,
> and yet think it is not inconsistent with monotheism if they also
> worship his servant (*Contra Celsum* VIII.12)

The writer of these words was a pagan, Celsus, the first to take up
the pen against Christianity. We have his words despite the loss of
his book, because a generation or so later the first great Christian
scholar, Origen, composed a blow by blow refutation of Celsus'
argument, quoting from him as he went along.

What offended Celsus, and the many ordinary educated people
he represented, was the refusal of Christians to join in the traditional
cultic celebrations of local communities and of the wider Empire.
He was quite happy to agree that there was one ultimate divine
being, along with most respectable philosophers of his day, Middle
Platonist and Stoic, but the general consensus was that this supreme
divinity delegated the day-to-day running of things to many lesser
divinities, gods and demons, and the safety and prosperity of the
state depended upon keeping the gods favourable. Maintaining the
traditional religious customs while adopting a more sophisticated
philosophical framework was the appropriate stance. Why couldn't
Christians behave like everyone else? All religions were variations
on the same thing anyway. Of course, Celsus knew the answer: they
had adopted the exclusiveness of the Jews, asserting that only the
one true God was to be worshipped. But they were not Jews, and
worse they compromised their position by treating Christ as God.
They were not monotheists after all.

It was in the context of apologetic and debate with outsiders that

Christian thinkers began to hammer out an answer to the logic which appeared to confute them: how could they proclaim one God and one Lord over against the gods many and lords many of the nations, without ending up with two gods? Despite their Jewish background, the theoretical issue never seems to have troubled Paul (to whose words in I Cor. 8 allusion has just been made) or the earliest believers. At first sight this seems very surprising, since we think of monotheism as the special feature of Judaism. But the God of the Jews had always had his servants, prophets, kings, angels, to reveal his will and proclaim his word, to be his 'sons'. The Messiah, or the supernatural agent of God who would officiate at the end of the world, was a special but perhaps not dissimilar case. It was the one God of Abraham, Isaac and Jacob that Jesus Christ revealed – Paul never questioned that, no matter how great the honours granted to the Son whom God had sent into the world, and whom God had raised from the dead. Of course he was higher than the angels, for God had delegated all his powers to him. To honour him was to honour God. Something like this attitude must account for the fact that the question was not an explicit issue for the writers of the New Testament.

But it rapidly became an issue. Jewish adherence to monotheism and high ethical standards was clearly respected by serious thinkers in the ancient world. The early Christian missions capitalized on this, spreading first among the God-fearers on the fringes of the synagogues. Faced with polytheism and idolatry, the revelation of the one true God and of the way of life he required, a revelation now finalized and universalized, in the life and teaching of Jesus Christ, became the basic message. Christianity was presented as a strict monotheism and a high morality, together with an assurance of life after death for the faithful. Little wonder that enquirers and doubters, not to mention opponents, would soon raise questions about the being and status of this Jesus Christ in relation to God.

A theoretical explanation we find first worked out in the writings of the Apologists, the second-century defenders of the faith, who wrote pleading for understanding and for recognition by the authorities, and answering current slanders. One, Justin Martyr, we have already met (see above pp. 26ff.), and in many ways he may be regarded as the most significant. It is interesting that he and the

pagan Celsus must have been approximate contemporaries. He orig-
inated in Samaria, but was clearly from a Hellenized if not Greek
family: he did the rounds of the philosophical schools, finding the
truth eventually in the Christian faith. He became a philosophical
teacher himself, travelling to Rome and there being martyred in
about AD 165. Genuine extant works include two Apologies,
addressed to the Emperor, and the *Dialogue with Trypho*, a debate
with a Jew about the meaning of the prophecies. Justin saw Christianity as the fulfilment not only of Judaism, but of all philosophy.

Philosophy provided him and other apologists with the language
and conceptual tools to explain how Jesus Christ was the revelation
of the one true God. In analysing rational discourse, Stoicism had
distinguished between the Logos in the mind of a person, the
Reason, and the Logos projected forth in speech, the Word. Stoicism
also regarded the Logos of each individual as related to the cosmic
Logos, the divine Reason or order permeating all things, indeed
generating all things. Justin exploited these ideas while adapting
them to a very different context. For Justin the one true God was
transcendent – Stoic pantheism was not an option. But Plato had
suggested that the Eternal Mind shaped matter in accordance with
the eternal Ideas or forms, and Platonists had developed his themes
into the concept of a transcendent divinity. Justin's account of things
implies that God always had his Logos or Reason within himself,
but in order to create he projected this Logos forth in creative speech
– for according to Genesis, God only had to speak his intention for
it to be accomplished. In this way, the first chapter of John's gospel
could be picked up and explained, along with other biblical passages
about wisdom like Proverbs 8. The Logos, the Word, was with God
in the beginning – indeed *was* God. This Logos was the only-
Begotten of God, the Word projected forth as the instrument
through whom God created, as the Wisdom who was beside him
fashioning all things, the Wisdom which orders and permeates all
that exists. It was this Word which came to the prophets – indeed
to Socrates and all genuine teachers of the truth, and in the last
days, it was this Word which was incarnate in Jesus Christ, fully
and finally revealing the truth of the one God, Creator of heaven
and earth.

This Logos-theology provided a rational explanation of how Jesus was the unique Son of God, different from all the sons of the gods in pagan mythology, both truly one with the one true God, and yet distinct. For Justin the really convincing proof of this lay in the fulfilment of prophecy. He knew miracles proved nothing, for Jesus was not the only miracle-worker of the ancient world. But prophecies were another matter. The ancient world was fascinated by oracles and their interpretation. Generals would not dare to fight a battle without consulting the omens, and governments tested policy by reference to collections of Sibylline oracles. Justin could amass lists of oracles and prophecies from the Jewish scriptures and show how they were fulfilled in Jesus Christ. So he proved that the prophecies were true, since they had been fulfilled, and that Christ was their true fulfilment. Given the crucial nature of this argument, it is hardly surprising that Justin felt obliged to tackle the problem that Jews did not agree with the Christian interpretation of their scriptures. In doing this he elaborated and developed an approach which had its roots in the New Testament, possibly in the teaching of Jesus himself.

Christian claims about Jesus were first couched in terms of the fulfilment of Messianic expectations. The various hopes and expectations developed out of the prophecies all tended to be focussed upon him, generating the many 'titles' applied to him by the early believers and found in the gospels and other New Testament writings. Quickly the process of searching the scriptures and compiling collections of 'testimonies' became established, and the triumphalist predictions were modified in the light of passages hinting at the suffering and death of the servant God would vindicate. Justin inherited all this, and contributed further to the process whereby Christians established the principle that the whole of the Jewish scriptures were really about Christ. The use of allegory and symbolism to interpret texts in terms of the realities of the Christian dispensation was commonplace. The result was a figure of 'many names', regarded fundamentally as the emissary prepared and sent by the providence of God. The Logos-theology gathered all this up into a coherent theory accounting for the preexistence and divinity of this unique revealer.

Other Apologists followed similar lines, some of them adopting Stoic technical terminology more explicitly than Justin. To some extent they had all been anticipated by the Jewish philosopher, Philo, who likewise had developed a concept of the Logos to elucidate the immanence of a God conceived as transcendent. Within the church, this theoretical development may well have enhanced the acceptability of John's gospel in a period in which its exploitation by Gnostics gave it a somewhat dubious reputation. Certainly the general acceptance of the gospel ensured the long-term importance of the doctrine, since it appeared to be clearly enunciated in its Prologue. Further development of ideas about how God and Jesus were related was either in reaction to or extension of these initial attempts at conceptualization.

Justin made much of the inspiration of the scriptures by the Holy Spirit, but in a sense the Logos-doctrine, by linking together the immanent activities of God, left little room for another source of inspiration. Irenaeus' understanding solved this difficulty by speaking of the Word and the Spirit as the two hands of God, both being instruments of the divine activity. Neither he nor Tertullian made much real advance on the fundamental approach of Logos-theology. The one God, who eternally had his Word and Spirit within him, 'became' a Trinity for the purposes of creation and providence, by generating his Word and breathing out his Spirit. This conception is often referred to as 'Economic Trinitarianism' (*oikonomia* being a Greek word meaning 'household management' which came to be used technically in early Christian theology to refer to the purposeful 'arrangements' God made, specifically to his providential ordering, and eventually to the incarnation in particular). Later this approach would prove inadequate, and it would be argued that God must be eternally and essentially Trinity – but much further debate was necessary for this to be recognized as necessary. If the origins of Logos-theology lie in apologetic, its further development was to be the result of internal argument, as Christians wrestled with those aspects they found unsatisfactory. Needless to say, in each dispute one side or the other lost out, and the losers were excluded as heretics. As time went on, the definition of truth became more and more precise and left less and less room for open enquiry. The extent to which this was an unfortunate legacy of the early struggle with Gnosticism, rather than a necessary process for refining the understanding of Christian truth, is a question to be kept in mind as we proceed.

While Victor was Pope in the last years of the second century, there appeared in Rome a certain Theodotus the Cobbler. According to the records we have, he insisted that Christ was a 'mere man' and Victor excommunicated him, but he caused a bit of a stir and got pupils and followers, including another Theodotus, the Banker. These people seem to have been concerned about the threat of Christian claims about Jesus to monotheism and suggested that this man, Jesus, proved perfect enough to be adopted by God as his Son. (Hence they are known as Adoptionists, though textbooks often refer to this heresy as Dynamic Monarchianism – see further below.)

They were not the only believers troubled by the issue of monotheism. Noetus of Smyrna posed problems around AD 200, claiming that Christ was the Father himself, that the Father himself was born and suffered and died. He began a long period of upset in the church at Rome in which the Logos-theology was resisted as being effectively Ditheism. The alternative proposed is often referred to as Modalist Monarchianism, and it seems to have gone through a number of subtly different versions, some more sophisticated than others. The most notorious teacher of this school was Sabellius. Our information largely comes from a hostile source, the anti-Pope Hippolytus, who suggested that Victor's successors, Zephyrinus and Callistus, were themselves infected by this heresy. To Zephyrinus he attributed the saying, 'I know one God, Jesus Christ; nor except him do I know any other that is begotten and susceptible to suffering', though he acknowledges that Zephyrinus was confused by reporting another occasion when he said, 'The Father did not die, but the Son'. Of Callistus, Hippolytus claims that as Pope he excommunicated Sabellius, but reports that he basically held no different opinions, charging Hippolytus and his associates with Ditheism. He perhaps tried to spell out a compromise position, for Hippolytus reports that Callistus alleged that the Logos was both Son and Father, and that God is one indivisible Spirit. Clearly the separation of God's Reason and the Word projected was being resisted. Father and Son could not be regarded as distinct persons: they are one and the same. All things are full of the Divine Spirit, and the Spirit is no different from the Father. There is one God not two, and the Father took flesh to himself and raised it to the nature of Deity, bringing it into union with himself. Thus Callistus avoided saying that the Father himself suffered, while resisting the division of the Godhead which Monarchians feared was the outcome of Logos-theology.

The charge of 'Patripassianism' was the most compelling point to be scored against these ardent monotheists. The implication of their teaching was that the transcendent God changed and suffered. He appeared in different Modes, as Father, then as Son, then as Spirit. He was himself incarnate, suffered and died. Tertullian wrote a treatise against this kind of teaching, *Against Praxeas*: who Praxeas was we are not sure, perhaps a local North African disciple of the heretics in Rome, though since Praxeas means 'Busy-body' it seems likely it is a pseudonym, possibly used to cover the fact that Tertullian was writing against the bishop of Rome himself. For Tertullian the attribution of change and suffering to God himself was simply a matter to be greeted with scorn. For him God in his transcendence was invisible, the Logos which proceeds from God was able to make God visible. He was like a ray projected from the sun, an offshoot which could mediate the transcendent. Without the Logos, God was reduced to a mythological character like Proteus who could change his form at will. And if Christ is the Father incarnate, to whom did he pray? And how did the universe keep running without him in charge? These people make much of the 'Monarchy' of God, Tertullian suggested, but we know perfectly well that an Emperor can share his monarchy with his son without dividing the Monarchy. With batteries of scriptural proofs, the pagan absurdities of the Modalist view were resisted, and it is the works of their opponents that have survived.

The result is that it is hard to do justice to their case, though one suspects that some of the arguments used against them are unfair. I doubt if they simply meant 'sovereignty' by monarchy, for *monarchia* could well refer to the idea of a single first principle: certainly it was what we refer to as monotheism which was at stake. It is interesting that people like Callistus use the idea of a single Divine Spirit, for in the twentieth century, the 'Oneness Pentecostals' have adopted the same kind of anti-Trinitarian theology, and can argue a very good case from the scriptures. As we have seen, Monarchianism had a sympathetic hearing in Rome. In fact the Western understanding of the Trinity would always tend to focus on the unity of God and resist tritheistic tendencies, by contrast with developments in Eastern Christianity. This difference is highlighted by an altercation in the 260s between Dionysius, bishop of Rome and Dionysius, bishop of Alexandria. The latter seems to have been hot against the Sabellians, and made certain statements concerning which complaints reached Rome. Backed by a synod, the Pope addressed the church at Alexandria, affirming the Divine Monarchy and objecting to its division into three substances, even though there is agreement that Sabellian identification of Father and Son is blasphemous. The Divine Triad is the one God of the Universe, and there are not three 'origins' or first principles. Even more to be resisted is the idea that the Son somehow came into being as a 'work' of God; his eternal unity with the Father and his generation from the Father's very own being alone does justice to what scripture affirms about him. The monotheistic principle must be defended against anything that would threaten it.

Dionysius of Alexandria replied defending himself. The correspondence reveals differences in emphasis, and possibly linguistic misunderstandings. To grasp the significance of this, we must go back a bit to trace the development of Logos-theology in the East. In the correspondence between the Dionysii, and in the recriminations of the later Arian controversy, it is quite clear that Sabellianism was the 'bête noir' of Eastern theology. Why?

The answer seems to lie in the widespread influence of the theology of the Alexandrian, Origen. That may seem a slightly problematic statement, since Origen's work was regarded with suspicion, even in his own day, and he would later be branded a heretic. Furthermore there is evidence of other views prevailing in Antioch: evidence of this has largely been suppressed in our sources, and evidence for christological developments outside the great centres in the third century, is largely lacking. Nevertheless, the kind of Logos-theology developed by Origen appears to furnish the background to the great Arian controversy which broke out as the Great Persecution receded before the conquering armies of an Emperor committed to supporting Christianity in the early fourth century.

Eusebius of Caesarea, the first historian of the church who wrote at the time of Constantine and lived through the great changes that took place then, suggests that there was a 'School' in Alexandria of an official kind, and a succession of scholarly heads of the school, of which one was Origen: Pantaenus, followed by Clement, followed by Origen, headed the so-called Catechetical School by appointment of the bishop. One suspects that this picture is a little distorted, and the nature of their relationship and activities was less direct and formal, more like a 'philosophical school' than a church membership class. There are interesting similarities between the views of Clement and Origen, though they never refer to one another and there are also considerable differences in emphasis. Both may be labelled 'Christian Platonists', but ironically the more overtly Platonist Clement became a Saint, and the more explicitly biblical and ecclesiastical Origen became a heretic, and in his own lifetime so incurred the displeasure of his bishop, that he had to transfer his library and his activities to Caesarea. (Eusebius inherited these resources a couple of generations later.) Both have been referred to as 'mystics', though the problem with such a label is one of meaningful definition; both have also been suspected of a kind of 'Gnosticism' though both accepted the Rule of Faith and argued against the doctrines of the Gnostic sects – Clement explicitly sought to foster 'true Gnostics', intellectual Christians who progressed further than the average believer, while Origen differentiated between teachings suitable for the more advanced, and those for the simple. Yet he used the fact that not just élite philosophers but even the simple are made good by Christianity as an argument against Celsus.

To do justice to the work of these Alexandrian scholars would take too much space here: but enough must be said to give something of a context for the development of Logos-theology in their thinking. For both, knowledge of God involved a process of abstraction – a stripping away of the distractions of the flesh, an asceticism both moral and intellectual, which allowed the soul to attend to the eternal world of Being, rather than the transient world of Becoming. Here there was a certain similarity with the spirituality of Gnosticism, but it was rooted in a more Platonic metaphysic, and did not involve the disparagement of the creation characteristic of Gnostic dualism. Indeed, the material world was invested with a kind of sacramental value, as the creation of a good God whose purpose was to provide a context in which fallen souls could be educated and he could reveal himself to those ready to receive knowledge of him. The

Logos of God was the mediator of his revelation, a revelation whose climax was the incarnation of the Logos in Jesus Christ. Indeed, Origen spelled out a scenario which gave a Christian answer to the philosophical questions about origins, about evil, about providence. Again there are similarities with Gnostic speculation, but also fundamental differences. The material universe was God's creation, though its occasion was the need to provide a 'reformatory' for such souls that had fallen from grace in the eternal spiritual world. Purification from fleshly desires and earthbound notions through moral and intellectual discipline would eventually lead to knowledge of the transcendent God, presently incomprehensible, but ultimately knowable through the direct intuition possible to a being with a kinship to the divine. For the immortal soul bears the image of God: Plato and Genesis cohered.

For Origen, as for contemporary Platonists, one fundamental issue was the problem of showing how the transcendent indivisible One related to the Many, yet being the ultimate ground of all Being. Typically the answer was that between the One and the Many was an intermediary substance, a One-Many or Indefinite Dyad, by which they meant a complex unity, sharing Oneness with the One and Multiplicity with the Many. Implicitly Origen seems to have identified God, the invisible, unnamable, untouchable, unchangeable, incomprehensible God of the Jewish scriptures, whom no one can see and live, with the ultimate One of Platonic thought. This God, though transcendent, is the Father and source of all Being, but he is eternal and unchangeable, so he always had his creation eternally alongside him, the multiplicity of 'intelligences', rational spiritual beings or *logikoi*, the angels and souls, the Many. The link between this one God and his many creatures was the Logos, who shared the unity of the Father and the multiplicity of his creatures. He was both the Reason of God himself, and the rationality of the whole created order. He has many 'names' because he is many things and performs many functions, as the principle underlying the creation and, after the Fall, effecting the redemption of all. He is eternally the Son of the Father, the mediating instrument generated by the Father to be his agent. Fundamentally, then, a 'hierarchy of being' is posited to explain all that exists: everything exists eternally, but depends utterly on the creativity of the one God, who is the source of all.

Within the totality of Origen's understanding, this hierarchical scheme worked well. It picked up the insights of Logos-theology and maintained monotheism by treating the Son as mediator of the one God. Origen insisted that only God is to be worshipped, and worship is offered to him *through the Son*. So the traditional Christian insistence that other beings, gods, angels or whatever, were *not* to be worshipped was firmly maintained, while the Son held a special place without undermining the monotheist emphasis. The Son was both one with the Father, and distinct, both in nature and function.

Maintaining both those sides of the equation, however, was to prove very difficult. Origen's scheme as a whole was altogether too sophisticated for most people, and elements in it were suspect. It was much easier to adopt the ideas of mediation, and the implicit hierarchy, and loosen the fundamental and necessary connection between the Logos and God. The Logos easily became a 'second God', sub-ordinate to the Father. Arius would be the one to press the logic home: God's Logos, his own internal Reason, was distinct from the Logos which he 'created' as his agent – the first and greatest of the creatures, but *not* essentially divine, since not ingenerate, unbegotten and without beginning. We will return to Arius later, but it is important to observe how wide was his sympathetic following in the Eastern church. On the whole people grasped the idea of the Logos as mediator, and were deeply suspicious of attempts to identify his being with that of God. Origen certainly bears some responsibility for this; his ideas about the eternal creation were never really taken up, and so his idea of the Son's eternal generation dropped out of sight until reclaimed by opponents of Arianism. Meanwhile the Eastern tendency to treat Father and Son as separate beings or substances is evident in the correspondence of the two Dionysii to which reference has already been made. Rome criticized the idea of three powers or three separate substances or *hypostases*: the precise Latin equivalent of *hypostasis* is *substantia*, and in the West this word was the long-standing term for the one divine substance shared by the Triad. Perhaps this linguistic fact contributed to the theological misunderstanding, but what is evident is that Dionysius of Alexandria remained anxious to avoid identifying Father and Son while acknowledging his derivation from the Father, a plant or shoot being different from its seed or root, and yet being absolutely of one nature with it. The same anxiety to maintain the distinct existence of the mediator is evident in the work of Eusebius of Caesarea and other Arian sympathizers. Eusebius as an apologist emphasizes monotheism and morality, but his christology of mediation enables him to insist on one God and one Lord without embarrassment. What he and his precursor, the Alexandrian Dionysius, had in common was a profound resistance to a Sabellian collapsing of the distinction between Father and Son.

When Dionysius of Alexandria was in extreme old age a controversy arose which reinforced, one suspects, the tendencies of Eastern Logos-theology. Unfortunately Eusebius never clarifies the teaching of the condemned bishop of Antioch, Paul of Samosata. He does much to blacken his name, socially, morally and politically, but precisely why his doctrines were condemned in 268 is far from clear. In subsequent debates, the accusation of following Paul is coupled with those of other heretics like Sabellius, and regarded as an extremely serious charge. Athanasius in defending the term *homoousios*, used in the Nicene Creed to exclude Arianism, had to explain away the fact that the Synod which condemned Paul, had apparently condemned the use of this term. If Origen's theology was the positive impetus to Eastern tendencies towards separation of Father and Son, opposition to Paul of Samosata seems to have been the negative reason for suspicion of Sabellian-type solutions. Yet was Paul a Sabellian?

Reports of Paul's teaching suggest at first sight that he was closer to the Adoptionists. The one anointed, the 'Christ', was a human being not the Logos. Mary did not give birth to the Logos – she was not before the ages nor is she older than the Word; she gave birth to a man like us, though better in every way. But clearly Paul accepted that this man was specially endowed with the Word itself and with the Wisdom of God – indeed was special because he was 'of the Holy Ghost'. His opponents accused him of treating Jesus Christ as no different from any other human being who participated in the Logos, but he seems to have rejected the analogy, and attempted to speak of a unique conjunction of the Logos himself with the human element 'from Mary'. So he was not quite a simple Adoptionist – here was no suggestion that divine adoption was a subsequent response to his perfection, taking place as divine power anointed him at baptism. The union was more constitutive than that, though perhaps rightly charged with being 'according to friendship and not according to substance'. Even more interesting are the post-Nicene explanations for the condemnation of *homoousios* – of one substance: 'in using this expression', explained Hilary, 'he declared the Father and Son were a solitary unit.' Athanasius suggests that Paul was suspicious of talk which suggested the derivation of one being from another, using materialist analogies. Whatever lies behind this, one thing seems clear: Paul was not happy with the typical Logos-theology, or a theology which suggested the divinity of Christ was that of a subordinate, mediating being. He was searching for a way of affirming the genuine humanity of Jesus Christ as a revelation of the real Logos or Wisdom of God himself. In the process he seems to have arrived at conceptions which sounded both Sabellian and Adoptionist. The resultant uproar sealed the fate of any subsequent Eastern theologian whose words sounded a Sabellian note. The opponents of Arius, such as Athanasius, Marcellus and others, were faced with this difficulty, and support they received in the West did not guarantee success in the East. Between them, Origen and Paul of Samosata had in different ways ensured that Eastern theology had a deep and endemic hostility to any kind of Modalism, and conceived of God and his relationship with the world in terms of a hierarchy with the 'one Lord Jesus Christ' having the nature, status and role of mediator between the 'one God' who was ultimately Father and source of all, and everything else that exists. The one Lord Jesus Christ was the incarnation of the pre-existent Logos, the creative instrument used by God to generate his creation and communicate with it. He was a second *hypostasis*, a distinct existence, never to be confused with the one ultimate, ingenerate God.

It was the Arian controversy which revealed the inadequacy of such an understanding, and that is why it has hovered over the discussion so far. It is time to look more closely at this crucial debate.

Arius was a priest in a suburb of Alexandria, an expounder of the scriptures, a popular teacher, but perhaps not really very significant had he not initiated a controversy which roused such feelings the whole world became involved. At one stage bishops were to protest at being labelled 'Arians' – they were bishops of the church, not followers of a minor priest. Later 'Arians' seem to have been sophisticated philosophers and logicians who developed these teachings way beyond anything Arius himself conceived of, and had little or no personal link with him. But the label stuck ... From the point of view of understanding the 'historical Arius' a great deal of careful analysis of slanted sources written at later stages in the debate is essential, and much recent scholarship has been concerned to try and produce a fairer account than the traditional versions passed on by the ancient moulders of church history. Here there is space only to explore the issues rather than trying to discern details or attribute responsibility. The fact is that once the dispute between Arius and his bishop became more than local, the majority of Eastern church leaders felt greater sympathy for moderate Arian views than for the anti-Arian position adopted at the Council of Nicaea and backed by Athanasius and the West. Politics certainly came into the whole story, the Emperor and his advisers simply wanting church unity as part of their programme to unite the Empire, but the fifty-year struggle is not simply explained in political terms. Nor is it fair to dismiss it, as the historian Socrates did a century later, as a wrangle over an iota: *homoousios* or *homoiousios*. There were profound theological issues at stake.

Arius was certainly a monotheist: he confessed one God, alone ingenerate or unbegotten, alone everlasting, alone unbegun, who begat an only-Begotten Son before eternal times through whom He made both the ages and the universe, perfect creature of God, not as one of the creatures. The Father alone is God, according to Arius; the Son is the first and greatest of the creatures. He is 'divine', one might say, but not God as God is God. There are therefore three *hypostases*, three existent beings, Father, Son and Spirit, but the Father is the Monad, the only true God: the others are derivative not ingenerate beings. Certainly the Monad cannot be divided as Sabellius suggested, speaking of a 'Son-and-Father', nor can the Son be regarded as a 'portion' of the Father, consubstantial with him. Such are the views expressed by Arius in a letter to his bishop, Alexander.

To some this language suggests that Arius' motivation was purely theoretical and philosophical, but other evidence suggests that Arius was a biblical literalist, and the language describing the Son as 'begotten' figures large in justification of his position. Others have recently stressed Arius' appeal to a view of salvation which sees 'Sonship' as attainable by all creatures, and the triumph of the Son of God over temptation as exemplary. For the consequence of treating the Son as a creature was to make him potentially *treptos* – changeable, therefore temptable, therefore able to prove that the conquest of sin and the attainment of righteousness are within creaturely grasp. But if this were attractive to some, it was the point at which many found they had to reject the Arian position, despite its apparent congruence with much else regarded as the traditional teaching of the church. The sources and motivation of the teaching of Arius himself is still under discussion, but its apparent similarity to the traditional hierarchical scheme, to what people like Eusebius of Caesarea had always believed and taught, is indisputable: indeed Eusebius got himself tarred with the Arian brush, and was hardly satisfied with the outcome of the Nicene Council. But Eusebius certainly rejected the idea that the Son might have sinned. In relation to traditional teaching, Arianism had its strengths, but also its fundamental weaknesses.

Exposing these weaknesses was largely the work of Athanasius in the great anti-Arian treatises written some decades after the Nicene Council. He was able to show that the whole hierarchical approach was actually undermined by Arius' kind of subordinationism. The Logos could no longer be the Mediator because in principle he shared nothing of the divine nature, except by grace. He was not *essentially* one with God. God's own internal Reason or Logos had no connection with the Logos he created. His was not the true divine Wisdom but only a kind of image of it. So he had no real knowledge of God and could not really reveal him. He was not essentially God's Son at all, simply a creature adopted by God as his agent. He could not communicate the divine, because he was not himself divine. This was inevitably the death-knell of a hierarchical approach: either the Logos was God or he was a creature and he could not be both. A new theological approach was inevitable. Athanasius' novel approach, which certainly owed something to the Monarchian-type of theology in the West, was deeply threatening to Eastern traditionalists, and they mostly settled for a position later referred to as 'semi-Arianism'. Of course the Logos was in some sense divine: some suggested he was 'like in substance' (*homoiousios*) though not identical in substance, as the Nicene *homoousios* seemed to imply.

So it was that the Council of Nicaea in 325 failed to resolve the issue, and for about fifty years, repeated attempts were made to replace the Nicene Creed with a more acceptable formula. A succession of 'Arian' Emperors made the process more difficult, but why should the Emperors have espoused the Arian cause if it had not looked potentially more successful than the Nicene in bringing peace and unity to the church in the East? Gradually through explanation, development and accommodation, a return to the Nicene formula became feasible and convincing to the majority. The result was the Council of Constantinople in 381, and the acceptance of the creed universally known as Nicene and used in liturgies both Eastern and Western.

Christianity affirmed one God. The one Lord was 'of the same substance' as the Father, one God identical in substance, action and will. Jesus was not the incarnation of a subordinate mediating being, but the revelation of the one true God. It really was God, God's self, who was born in the Lord Jesus Christ. But such a definition of his being could not be allowed to imply a Sabellian understanding, nor was it easy to explain how a being so defined could become incarnate. Both Trinitarian doctrine and christology had to be refined in the light of the new Nicene theology.

4

The Holy Spirit and the Holy Catholic Church

The explicit agenda in the Arian controversy concerned the nature of the relationship between the Son/Logos and the Father/God. But the implicit agenda was the nature of salvation. Athanasius' most persistent criticism of Arianism was linked with the ideas outlined at the end of chapter 2: 'He became human (man) that we might become divine (god)', he insisted, and argued that if he were to effect our *theopoiēsis* (divinization or deification), the Logos must himself be divine. These points we will pursue further in the last chapter, but it is significant that the crucial Arian debate, and the subsequent debates to be followed in this chapter and the next, constantly pre-suppose the emotional investment of people who saw their salvation threatened by the ideas they opposed.

The struggle to affirm the full divinity of the Word was rapidly succeeded by a parallel struggle to affirm the full divinity of the Holy Spirit. Through both these struggles the West in a sense looked on while the East refined its thinking. As we have already noted (p. 37 above), a form of explicit Trinitarianism already existed in the thinking of Irenaeus and Tertullian, and on the whole the West had no difficulty in embracing a theology of Trinity-in-Unity. The hierarchical tendencies of Eastern thought, however, made the issues more complex, and in a sense Logos-theology itself left no room for the Spirit, for the Word of God, active in creation and revelation, pre-empted the Spirit's biblical functions.

Nevertheless, 'triadic' formulae are found in the New Testament and remained in use in the church's liturgical and confessional language, despite there being little attempt to conceptualize the relationships. Baptism generally followed the Matthaean commission, using the three-fold name (see Matt. 28.19). Justin made much of the prophetic Spirit, the Spirit traditionally being associated particularly with the inspired oracles which pointed in riddles to the manner of the future coming of the Christ. But the New Testament suggests that the Spirit was not just the inspirer of the written oracles of the past. There was a dramatic outbreak of prophecy in the life of the earliest church associated with the gift of the Spirit. There is some evidence that 'prophets' still played their part in the life of the second-century church, at least prior to the Montanist movement.

The Montanist movement was a controversial new outbreak of prophecy. Reports associate with it 'strange sounds', perhaps a resurgence of glossolalia, and predictions of the imminent arrival of the new Jerusalem. It arose in Phrygia (Asia Minor), but in time spread beyond its immediate locality, even to Rome and North Africa. Irenaeus has a fairly tame reaction to it, and in some ways it seems little different from the apocalyptic and visionary type of Christianity found in much of the New Testament and in the Millenarian groups of the second century which resisted Gnostic influence (Millenarians believed in the imminent 1000 year reign of Christ on earth as predicted in Revelation). Tertullian would become a Montanist, attracted by the movement's 'puritan' and rigorist life-style.

Montanus and his female associates, Priscilla and Maximilla, initiated this New Prophecy, as it was called. At Ardabau, Montanus was 'filled with spiritual excitement and suddenly fell into a trance and unnatural ecstasy', according to a long report quoted by Eusebius in his *Church History*. Epiphanius reports that Priscilla said, 'Christ came to me in the likeness of a woman, clad in a bright robe, and he planted wisdom in me and revealed that this place (Pepuza) is holy, and that here Jerusalem comes down from heaven', while Maximilla claimed that 'after me shall be no prophetess any more, but the consummation'. Fasting and virginity were preached. They claimed many martyrs.

Montanus, however, is sometimes referred to as 'the Paraclete', and this may be a hint that Montanism was no innocent, basically orthodox, apocalyptic and charismatic movement, resisted because the institutionalized church could no longer cope with the uncontrollable prophetic element, but rather a claim about the incarnation of the Paraclete. But he is also supposed to have said, 'I am the Lord God Almighty, dwelling in man. It is neither angel nor ambassador, but I, God the Father, who am come', which might suggest that the theology of the movement was 'modalist'. Maximilla is quoted as saying, 'Hear not me, but hear Christ', and also 'I am driven away like a wolf from the sheep. I am not a wolf; I am word and spirit and power.' Had a proper distinction between the Spirit, the Father and the Word been lost? It seems unlikely that doctrinal issues of this kind were at stake, since they do not figure, as far as we can tell from the limited evidence, among the arguments at the time, and if there were recognizably unorthodox doctrines of this kind, Tertullian's later attraction to the movement is odd. Contemporary objections to Montanus and his associates are couched in terms of a dispute about the manner of inspiration, and perhaps this is the most significant aspect to explore further.

'Behold a man is as a lyre', said Montanus, 'and I fly over it like a plectrum. The man sleeps, and I remain awake. Behold it is the Lord that stirs the hearts of men, and gives men hearts.' Now the 'lyre' image was a Hellenistic commonplace. The Delphic Oracle and the Sibyls were 'taken over' by the god who spoke in his own person through them. Ecstasy, trance and 'divine madness' were associated with this process. The documents Eusebius quotes against Montanus, and the arguments produced by others like Origen, all focus on the appropriate understanding of inspiration. People thought Montanus was 'possessed, a demoniac in the grip of a spirit of error, a disturber of the masses'. Far from being the Holy Spirit, it was a 'spirit of deception' and 'unnatural ecstasy'. 'They cannot point to a single one of the prophets under either the Old Covenant or the New who was moved by the Spirit in this way', said their accusers. For Origen, inspiration did not mean the evacuation of the prophet's mind, but rather a heightening of the prophet's consciousness. No wonder then that the church used against this movement the New Testament warnings to test the spirits and avoid false prophets. Most of the extant sayings suggest not so much a specific incarnation of the Paraclete as a claim by one or other of the three to be 'taken over' by the Spirit, or the divine Word or Power; and the loose language is probably typical of the second-century church, rather than being specifically Modalist.

The dating of this movement is not altogether clear: Eusebius suggests the outbreak occurred in AD 172, Epiphanius in 156–7. Probably Epiphanius is right, and Eusebius refers to the period in which the church began to deal with the problem. It was in the early third century that Rome and Tertullian were exercised about the movement. Tertullian accuses Praxeas of 'crucifying the Father and putting the Paraclete to flight', linking his opponent's resistance to Montanism with his Modalist views: it could well be Roman resistance to the New Prophecy which occasioned that remark.

Despite resistance to Montanism and a consequent reduction of ecstatic and prophetic phenomena, the church did not abandon belief in the Holy Spirit's activity. As the canon of scripture was formed, the suggestion gained acceptance that nothing could be added to the inspired Word contained therein – indeed, resistance to Montanism may have occasioned that development – but that did not close off the possibility of the Spirit being at work in the life of the church, for only one inspired by the Spirit could read and interpret the Word aright. At baptism, false spirits were exorcized and the Holy Spirit received. The Spirit inspired and sanctified the church, its members, its sacraments, its priests and teachers. That this was God at work in the life of the church was taken for granted. The 'Triad' is named in the late second century, and early in the third, Tertullian translated it into the Latin *Trinitas*. Like Irenaeus, he conceives of Word and Spirit as the inner Reason and Wisdom of God himself projected forth, each being derivatives of the Father, each at work in the world and in particular in the Christian community. This tendency to give the Word and the Spirit a mediating role, however, facilitated the hierarchical views of the East, and placing Logos and Spirit on a kind of 'ladder of existence' made the difference between Spirit and angel difficult to specify. It was natural, therefore, that the Arian controversy about the Logos should produce a parallel debate about the Being of the Holy Spirit.

So round about 360, Athanasius found himself obliged to answer letters from Serapion, Bishop of Thmuis, which spoke of 'certain persons who had forsaken the Arians on account of their blasphemy against the Son of God, yet oppose the Holy Spirit, saying he is not only a creature but actually one of the ministering spirits, and differs from the angels only in degree'. The debate seems to have centred on scriptural texts, and Athanasius calls them Tropici since they explained biblical texts which were awkward for their position *tropikōs* or metaphorically. They also argued that if the Spirit were of God, he must either be another Son, which would not do since the Son is Only-begotten and can have no brother, or must be a Grandson of the Father! Athanasius argues that the Spirit is the spirit of Christ within us, and his divinity is therefore the correlate of Christ's divinity. Furthermore our sanctification and deification depends on the work of the Spirit within us, and if the Spirit is a creature, he could not make us divine. As in the debate with the Arians, the argument is based on what is necessary for salvation to be real, and it leads to uncompromising statements about the whole Triad being one God.

About ten to fifteen years later, though apparently independently, Basil of Caesarea faced similar opponents. In his treatise *On the Holy Spirit*, he was responding to the charge of innovation in the form of doxology: he said, 'Glory be to the Father with the Son together with the Holy Spirit' instead of 'through the Son', 'in the Holy Spirit'. He justified this, claiming that both forms were traditional and both in accordance with church doctrine. All three were co-worshipped and co-glorified. In its liturgy, the church accorded equal honour and dignity to Son and Spirit as to the Father, which was appropriate since all shared the same divine nature, and all were involved in the divine activities of creation and salvation. The Spirit was particularly associated with the divine work of sanctification in the sacraments. As the Macedonians or 'Spirit-fighters' pressed the case, and confusion continued, some, as Gregory of Nazianzus indicates, considering the Spirit to be a 'force' (*energeia*), others a creature, others God, others refusing to make up their minds on the grounds that scripture is vague, Basil became more definite still, but he never took the step of applying *homoousios* to the Spirit. Nor did the expanded clause concerning the Spirit found in the Nicence Creed adopted at Constantinople in 381 (see above p. 14).

Soon, however, the consubstantiality and Godhead of the Spirit were openly and explicitly claimed, and to avoid the charge that the Father therefore had two sons, the manner of the Spirit's derivation was described as 'procession' (on the basis of John 15.26) rather than 'generation'. So the way was now clear for the development of a truly Trinitarian understanding of the one God, and though anticipated to some extent by Athanasius, it was the Cappadoceans, Basil, with his friend, Gregory of Nazianzus, and his brother, Gregory of Nyssa, who provided for the East the definitive expositions of such a doctrine.

Since *homoousios* defined their unity, it was natural that the term *ousia* should be used for what they had in common. To reduce all three to one *hypostasis*, however, had long had Sabellian implications for the East, for *hypostasis* implied individual subsistence. The problem had been that *ousia* and *hypostasis* were used synonymously – hence the resistance to Athanasius' doctrine, influenced as it probably was by the West (see pp. 45, 47 above). Someone, possibly Didymus the Blind (the phrase is first found in a treatise attributed to Basil but clearly not his), had the brilliant idea of distinguishing the meaning of these two words for 'substance' so as to produce the formula, *Three Hypostases in One Ousia*.

With their Platonic tendencies, the Cappadocians then explained the relationship in terms of the universal and the particular: so that as Peter, James and John were of the same substance, namely humanity, so Father, Son and Spirit were distinct *hypostases* sharing the same *ousia*. To us the problem is evident: how is this different from tritheism? That charge Gregory of Nyssa sought to meet, but already Basil had insisted that number is not applicable to divinity, nor is the divine being divisible into parts: in relation to God, you cannot add one and one and one to make three. The unity is real not notional, because God is inherently simple and incomposite. In other words, a generic unity is only the starting-point of understanding, the divine being having characteristics fundamentally different from discrete creatures.

So, they suggested, the three are differentiated by their 'manner of being', as 'ingenerate', 'generated', and 'proceeding', or by their relationships of 'paternity', 'sonship' and 'sanctifying power'; but they are united in their substance, activities and will. The whole Trinity is Creator, Saviour, Sanctifier, all three identified with the activities of each and none having a distinct operation of his own. The whole Trinity is eternal and exists simultaneously and always as one Godhead in three hypostases: in other words this is an 'essential

Trinitarianism' by contrast with the 'economic Trinitarianism' of Irenaeus and Tertullian (see above p. 37). God does not change, so he must have always been Trinity and did not 'become' Trinity for reasons of the 'economy'. Furthermore, God cannot lie, since he is the very principle of truth: so if he is revealed as Trinity, that revelation must correspond to his eternal reality.

Yet, for all that, the Cappadocians insisted that God remains beyond definition, beyond our language and categories, in principle incomprehensible because he is infinite. The Trinity must be affirmed, therefore, as a proper Mystery. If they seem very confident of knowing all about God, in fact that claim to know all about God was their chief objection to the doctrines of their extreme Arian opponents (the Eunomians). It was altogether too easy to define God in terms of the 'ingenerate' and then argue logically from that to a fundamentally limited view of his nature, and so, ironically, in the interests of monotheism espouse a doctrine of three beings of different ontological status, in effect, a polytheism. So finding the Trinitarian 'mean' between the simple monotheism of the Jews and the proliferating polytheism of the Greeks became the way to Christian truth, and to acknowledging the essentially mysterious being of God.

Despite a clearer grasp at an earlier date that a Trinitarian doctrine was necessary, the West was not unaffected by what was happening in the East, and by the time of Augustine the 'economic' Trinitarianism of Tertullian had also given way to an 'essential' Trinitarianism. The West had to respond to the situation brought about by the Arian controversy by showing that its tradition was not Sabellian, and by trying to persuade the Easterners that the Nicene formula was more appropriate than any other. By doing this, Hilary of Poitiers, and then later the Christian Neoplatonist, Victorinus, prepared the ground for Augustine's classic exposition of the doctrine, *De Trinitate*, compiled between 399 and 419. The terminology used since Tertullian, 'One God in Three Persons', or one *substantia* in three *personae*, remains, but Augustine was profoundly aware of the difficulties with this terminology: he preferred 'essence' to 'substance', and would only use 'persons' because otherwise he would have nothing to say at all. For him the 'social' concept of the Trinity is quite out of place: there is only One God. Father,

Son and Spirit are not in any sense separate individuals. They 'indwell' one another: each one is infinite, eternal, almighty, perfect, etc., but there are not three infinites, three eternals, three almighties, three perfects, etc., only one. Their operation, action and will is one and inseparable.

How then is each to be characterized as distinct? They are distinct neither in substance nor accident, but in relation, Augustine suggests, as begetting, being begotten and proceeding. So far what Augustine says seems very similar to the Cappadocians, but his analogies indicate the difference in emphasis. The relationship of universal and particular is not for him a suitable way of approaching the matter. The experience of being, knowing and willing provides a better approach. So his preferred analogies are psychological, the 'inner' trinity of memory, understanding and will in the mind, or the mind's knowledge of and love of itself. 'The image of the Trinity is One Person'. Yet that is not enough – for the Trinity is Three Persons and yet more inseparably one than the mind. Another approach is to suggest that perception involves the trinity of the perceiving subject, the perceived object and the perception which links them. Somewhat parallel, though not central to Augustine's thought, is the hint that God is love, and love cannot exist without the possibility of a distinction between the lover, the beloved and the love that exists between them. The Spirit, being as it were that mutual love, issues from both Father and Son. All such attempts, however, are only initial steps towards understanding the nature of the Trinity. The 'relations' that constitute the distinctions cannot be conceived as relations between discrete individuals. The 'Persons' 'coinhere', and all analogies only help us to see in glass darkly.

There remains then a subtle difference in emphasis between East and West, though both seek to do justice to the essential Being of God as a mysteriously simple yet complex unity. Already, too, we can see tendencies which will lead to the mediaeval division between the Pope and the Eastern Orthodox churches: for the East regards the Father as the 'fount' of the Godhead eternally 'producing' both Son and Spirit, whereas Augustine stresses the Father and Son as mutually the 'source' of the Spirit (see note on the '*filioque*' at the end of this chapter). But clearly by the end of the fifth century, a more or less common doctrine of God has emerged.

The creeds (Apostles' and Nicene) stated the essential components of that doctrine, though never spelt it out conceptually. The so-called Athanasian Creed (a Latin product of the late fourth or early fifth century, easily accessible for interested readers in the *Book of Common Prayer*) set out to do precisely that. It provides an intellectual challenge, or enunciates meaningless paradox, according to your point of view. It is a succinct summary of the classic Trinitarian position reached by Augustine, though for most worshippers it cannot begin to express the spiritual dynamics of their understanding of God. Some of the discussions we have reviewed can likewise be seen as logical exercises, dry as dust. But that is to miss the passions of the controversies, fired as they were by a concern to do justice to what God had revealed and given in and through Christ. It is also to miss the fact that meditation on a well-developed exposition of the doctrine of the Trinity is more than a teasing of the mind: it enables an imaginative grasp of what is involved in knowing and understanding one who is no anthropomorphic idol, but the living transcendent God of biblical and Christian tradition. For Eastern Orthodoxy, the mystery of the Trinity is at the heart of the liturgy. It is a pity that nowadays so much Western church life prefers not to attend to this doctrine too closely.

Paying attention to the doctrine of the Holy Spirit led to the formulation of a truly Trinitarian concept of God. But the final clause of the creed links with the Holy Spirit, the one holy catholic and apostolic church, along with baptism for the remission of sins, the resurrection and eternal life. This expresses the Spirit's 'sphere of activity'. Though the whole Trinity is involved, it is the 'proper' work of the Spirit to effect salvation through the church and the sacraments. What then is the nature of this community, the church, which the Spirit forms and sanctifies?

This, too, was the subject of controversy in the early centuries. At first, as we can see from the New Testament, the Christians saw themselves as the 'holy elect', those purified and ready, awaiting the consummation of God's kingdom which was imminent. The surprising thing was that Gentiles were included in the 'righteous remnant' to be redeemed on the Final Day of Judgment, but otherwise these little communities were 'the Israel of God', the 'first-fruits', the 'nuclei' if you like, of the kingdom to come, and their members were guaranteed resurrection and salvation by being in Christ. Immediate expectations were unfulfilled, and, as we can see from the First Epistle of John, the church very quickly became vexed by the problem of those who claimed to be 'perfect' and sinless, since their baptism had sanctified them. 'If we say we have no sin, we are deceived and there is no truth in us. If we confess our sin, he is faithful and righteous to forgive us our sin and cleanse us from all unrighteousness' (I John 1.8–9). Those are the words of one who has to clarify the point that the End is not yet, and the elect are not yet holy.

But even as the church came to terms with living in the world, the old ideology did not entirely fade. At baptism, the world, the flesh and the devil were renounced, and a radical break expected. So post-baptismal sin was a problem. Public penance came to be acceptable for the inevitable minor lapses. But a close-knit persecuted community could not in any case tolerate any disloyalty, and those who committed apostasy, murder or adultery, the Jewish 'sins committed with a high hand', could find no forgiveness after baptism. Martyrdom sometimes counted as a second baptism, or baptism in blood – indeed, the virtue of the martyrs, like that of Christ, could expiate the sins of others. But 'holiness' was the mark of the 'elect', only the 'pure' could participate in the eucharist, and 'sinners' were excluded. Some were more morally 'rigorist' than others: Clement of Alexandria was distinctly more tolerant of worldly comforts than Tertullian. But there was a general sympathy towards strictness and a refusal of moral compromise.

The crisis provoked by the Decian persecution is an indication of how this ideology lived on. During the first part of the third century, the church seems to have prospered in the towns and cities around the Mediterranean – it even began to acquire property. There was growing social acceptance, and numbers apparently increased dramatically. Some modern accounts speak of many being 'nominal' Christians, but that is surely to read back our situation into a very different context. What is likely, however, is that some new converts never really appreciated the exclusive claims of Christ. The popular view was that you went to different gods for different benefits: if you wanted healing, you'd go to Aesclepius, and in the same way, if you wanted immortality, you'd go to Christ. So they treated baptism as being initiated into mysteries which through eucharistic feeding guaranteed eternal life. But at the core of the church were those who still looked for absolute commitment, and absolute purity.

The emperor Decius had problems, both economic and military. The Empire was threatened. Why had Rome's greatness gone? The natural answer was the breakdown of Rome's traditional piety towards the gods that had made her great. Whether deliberately singling out the Christians or not, Decius promulgated an edict in AD 250 which would damage Christians alone. Everyone in the Empire was to offer sacrifice or incense to the Roman gods, except Jews who were exempt by reason of a long-standing special relationship, dating back to a treaty between Rome and the Maccabees, which ensured that their religious scruples were upheld under Roman law. Christians had long since regarded themselves as a 'third race', neither Jews nor 'Greeks' (a cultural rather than racial term), and this edict made the point dramatically. Christians could not conform.

But many either did, or pretended to, getting hold of certificates to show that they had. The 'puritans' in the church were horrified. The 'lapsed' were desperate to be received back into communion, but were excluded; they were apostates. The situation is entirely understandable if these 'weaker brethren' had the attitudes outlined above: it would account both for their easy failure and their demands for re-admission. They had not realized their response to the edict meant their eternal salvation was at stake.

The correspondence of Cyprian, bishop of Carthage in North Africa, shows us the seriousness of the crisis. The hard-liners certainly had tradition behind them, but gradually Cyprian realized that compassion was demanded by his pastoral responsibilities, and he worked towards an episcopal agreement to establish terms of penance, and even re-admission if someone were on their death-bed. To some extent events forced his hand. For meanwhile he was involved in a power-struggle. Who had the authority to 'bind and loose', to absolve sin? God alone could forgive. But in the prisons were the 'confessors' awaiting trial for their refusal to conform to the edict. The word 'confessor' or 'martyr' simply means 'witness' and clearly these people were not yet dead; but they were bound to suffer for their stand, either by paying the death penalty or by being condemned to slavery in the mines or to row triremes (i.e. in the Roman navy). Imprisonment was not a punishment under Roman Law, and those held awaiting trial were supported by relatives and friends. Christians therefore had access to their 'confessing' heroes, and it was widely believed that the blood of the martyrs was expiatory. The 'lapsed' now produced more certificates, certificates of forgiveness given them by compassionate confessors, and with these tickets, demanded re-admission to the sacrament. Did the bishop have the power to refuse?

In a sense Cyprian had already less moral authority than the confessors because he had gone into hiding. This was justifiable: preachers had long insisted that it was as wrong to seek the glory of martyrdom as to commit suicide, and he had his pastoral responsibilities to consider. But the charismatic authority of the martyrs was bound to seem greater than the authority of an absent fugitive. Furthermore, the office of bishop had probably not yet developed the kind of authority it soon acquired, partly through Cyprian's own actions and arguments. So the church in Carthage was torn between those who would adopt an entirely lax policy, and those who wished to reaffirm the old rigorist stance: Cyprian stood for discipline with compassion.

This situation we find repeated all around the Roman world, in Alexandria, in Rome itself. Indeed, in Rome the bishop was martyred. A rigorist, Novatian, protested against the election of Cornelius, and had himself consecrated as bishop. The Novatianist, 'denomination' lasted centuries, and the church historian Socrates, writing in the fifth century, registers his respect for their high standards of purity. But Cyprian and Cornelius moderated the old rigorist views, and councils of bishops drew up suitable systems of penance and rules for re-admission, suggesting that the church was a school for sinners rather than the sanctuary of the saved elect. In the conditions of this imperfect world, the 'holiness' of the elect could not realistically be maintained, as the author of I John had realized long before. Wheat and tares were bound to grow together, and the Ark contained both clean and unclean beasts.

The church's self-understanding was challenged by these events, and if its ideal of purity was compromised, its assertion of its unity was reinforced in the face of its actual disintegration. Novatian had torn the seamless robe of Christ, and that was no better than heresy. Cyprian wrote a treatise *On Unity*, asserting that outside the church, there is no salvation. 'He who leaves the church of Christ attains not to Christ's rewards. He is an alien, an outcast, an enemy. He can no longer have God for a Father who has not the church for a mother. If any man was able to escape who was outside the ark of Noah, then will that man escape who is out of doors beyond the church' (*De Unitate* 6). Novatian and his followers were excluded.

It was this exclusion policy that enabled the church to retain belief in its unity, and so mislead later historians into thinking that disunity and denominationalism is largely a phenomenon of the post-Reformation world. The early church claimed to be both one and holy, but in practice the church on earth was neither. In theory, however, the unity of the church was now vested in the communion of its legitimate bishops throughout the Empire. The Roman succession from the apostles guaranteed the doctrinal tradition, as Irenaeus had earlier stressed (see above p. 24), and Cyprian relates the authority of the episcopate to Christ's commissioning of Peter (Matt. 16.18–20). The bishops (rather than the martyrs) had the Christ-given power to 'bind and loose'. So as councils of bishops came to disciplinary decisions on matters such as suitable terms of penance, bishops acquired increasing control, the unity, catholicity and apostolicity of the church being vested in the episcopal college. There is one God, Christ is the one Lord, there is one Holy Spirit, and one bishop in the (local) church; whoever is not in communion with the bishop is outside the church, and the bishop is the bond of unity both in the local congregation and through his membership of the corporate episcopate diffused throughout the world.

Fifty years later, a closely parallel controversy arose, again in North Africa, with the Diocletianic persecution. This time the emperor's edict was clearly aimed at the Christian leadership; the requirement was the surrender of copies of the scriptures for burning. A new bishop was elected, but some accused one of his consecrators of being a 'traditor', one who had handed over the scriptures. So a certain Donatus became the leader of a church body which claimed to be the true church, indeed the real inheritor of the legacy of Cyprian. The issue of 'holiness' was again central. One who was not visibly holy could pass on the pollution, and so the whole succession from an unholy priest would be corrupted. A century later Augustine was still struggling for unity, claiming that the Donatists could not be the true church since they were not 'catholic' – they were only local and not in communion with the churches elsewhere in the world. Eventually he justified the use of force and state persecution to bring the Donatists into line. That was a fateful move.

These were not the only schisms: splits happened in Egypt, Antioch and elsewhere without there being major doctrinal differences, though often the distinction between heresy and schism was blurred. Some schisms were the result of personality clashes, some accusations of heresy were made on moral grounds, and as we have seen, some splits had doctrinal implications, if not for the central affirmations of the creeds, certainly for the church's claims about itself. Whatever the root cause, schism involved refusal to share communion, and indeed raised difficulties about the nature of the sacraments: was the baptism, or ordination, of a Novatianist or Donatist valid, or did the sacrament need to be repeated if they sought reconciliation with the church? On this issue, Cyprian had taken a strict line, as might be expected: rites performed outside the church had no validity. The Donatists adopted this policy for themselves, refusing to recognize the sacraments of the 'catholics'. But Cyprian and Cornelius' successor at Rome, Stephen, had in fact fallen out over this issue, and Augustine takes a less clearcut position.

For Augustine, as for Stephen, the grace of God could not be dependent upon the priest's purity of character. Stephen argued that baptism performed with the correct Trinitarian formula was baptism and need not be repeated. All that was necessary was the laying on of the bishop's hands to confirm the baptism and communicate the gift of the Spirit. Augustine argued that properly performed sacraments according to orthodox practice were valid and did not need to be repeated, but they had no effect, indeed 'profited them nothing because they had not charity'. They only became efficacious when the recipient was in unity, love and communion with the true church. Thus he tried to persuade Donatists to seek reconciliation, insisting that those who returned should be embraced in the unity of the Spirit and the bond of peace, and accorded the status they held before in the Donatist church.

Cyprian's doctrine of the church was consistent but narrow: the operation of the Spirit was confined to an episcopally defined community. Augustine had a wider perception of God's providential operating within the world, though by his definitions sacramental efficacy becomes rather impersonal in the interests of ensuring that God is not hampered by the inadequacies of sinful ministers. Nevertheless, the focus of Augustine's doctrine of the church rests on the communion and love of a community which is the Body of Christ. Love is therefore the essential sign of unity. It is tragic that his decades of frustration with the Donatists, coupled with government pressures, drove him to betray his vision, justify it though he would on the grounds that it was for the Donatists' own good, and Christ's parable had spoken of 'compelling them to come in' to the feast – in fact, parental love involves chastisement and compulsion.

For all the splits and controversies, the final clause of the creeds expressed the universal ideals of one holy, catholic and apostolic church, united by the bond of love and peace, in the power of the Spirit, effecting salvation, and bestowing resurrection and eternal life. The kind of ideas the early church had about salvation, resurrection and eternal life will be explored in the final chapter.

Note on the 'filioque'

The Orthodox churches of the East and the Roman Catholic church of the West parted company in the Middle Ages. In 1054 the Papal Legate excommunicated the Patriarch of Constantinople; even more damaging was the sack of Constantinople by crusaders in 1204. The Greek- and Latin-speaking churches had long been losing contact, and these events provided the occasion for severance of communion.

A number of minor issues figured large at the time, but lasting problems have centred around two major issues, Papal primacy and the *filioque* (Latin, meaning 'and the Son'). According to the Western version of the Nicene Creed, the Spirit 'proceeds from the Father *and the Son*', but the Eastern church has always regarded this as an addition lacking the authority of an ecumenical council. The two issues are therefore related: the addition, though local to Spain in origin, did eventually receive papal authority and was adopted universally in the Western church, passing to the Protestant churches at the Reformation. The issue still looms large in ecumenical discussions between East and West.

Some minimize the theological issues posed by the addition, but others take them more seriously. Controversy certainly exaggerated the minimal differences between the Cappadocians and Augustine, these being the authorities to which East and West appealed. Eastern theology made a clear distinction between the 'eternal procession' and the 'temporal mission' of the Spirit, the first referring to inner Trinitarian relationships, the latter to the 'economy'. They agreed that as far as the latter was concerned, the Spirit 'proceeded from the Father and the Son', but when it came to the former, on the authority of the Cappadocians, they maintained that the Father was the 'source' or 'fount' of the Godhead: the Father is 'cause', the Son and Spirit 'caused'. The Western doctrine, they feared, either retained a hierarchical (and therefore Neoplatonist) Trinity, or failed to distinguish the *hypostases* adequately. This led to a tendency to see the Spirit as merely the instrument of the Son, and a failure to do justice to his continuing operation in the world.

Procession from Father and Son could certainly claim the precedent of Augustine, and to him the West appealed. But Augustine had stressed the mutual and equal relations between Father, Son and Spirit, hoping to protect rather than endanger this by treating the Spirit as the 'bond' between Father and Son, proceeding from both. He also preserved alongside this the 'monarchy' of the Father as 'cause' of the Trinity, and stated that from him the Spirit principally proceeded. The Cappadocian view was hardly different: the Father was 'source', but the Spirit is 'out of God' and 'of Christ', 'out of the Father through the Son'; they recognized him as Spirit of God and Spirit of Christ. It was the development of later Western apologetic, suggesting that the Spirit proceeds from both 'as from one principle' that created insuperable difficulties.

Much Western philosophical theology can certainly be charged with a tendency to defend an a-Trinitarian theism, and much popular Christianity in the West fails to embrace the doctrine. On the other hand, Islam was in part a monotheistic reaction against a virtual tritheism in Eastern Christianity. Such broad generalizations are inevitably over-simplifications, but historic differences in emphasis between East and West can hardly be discounted. Whether those differences have really been so fundamental as to justify continued separation, however, is a question that must be addressed in this ecumenical age.

5

The Son of God Incarnate

We have seen how the new Nicene theology required refinement of the doctrine of the Trinity; it also necessitated further refinement of christology. Tertullian had been able to speak of the Logos being the visible form of the invisible, and pre-Nicene theology in general had tended to see the Logos as a Being capable of mediating between the transcendent One God and the multiplicity of creation. But once it was agreed that the Logos was 'of the same substance' as God the Father, he could no longer so easily be involved with the world of the visible, the corporeal, the changeable, the passible. Like the Father he had all the attributes of radical transcendence.

The debate with Arius involved discussion of these issues. It is evident from the works of Athanasius that Arius argued from texts in the gospels which suggested the weakness or ignorance of Christ to the 'creatureliness' of the Logos, despite his belief that the Logos was a pre-existent supernatural being, indeed the first and greatest of God's creatures through whom everything else was made. This was because he presupposed that incarnation meant that the real 'person' was the Logos within the 'flesh' of Jesus. Since many in the ancient world assumed that in the case of any human being, the real person was the eternal, immortal 'soul' within the 'flesh', such an understanding was not recognized as 'docetic' – indeed, it seemed natural and was probably inevitable. The Logos replaced the soul in the case of Jesus.

Reading Athanasius' reply to Arius, it soon becomes evident that he shared the same assumptions. Faced with Jesus weeping at Lazarus' tomb, being tired and thirsty at the well in Samaria, and not knowing the time of the End, Athanasius attributes these creaturely weaknesses to the 'flesh', refusing to deduce from them that the Logos himself had a creaturely nature. In the incarnation, the Logos submitted himself to the weaknesses of the 'flesh'; he suffered because it was 'his flesh', though he remained impassible in his essential being. This has been described as a 'space-suit' christology.* In one tell-tale passage, Athanasius even admitted that he 'imitated our condition', though he would have strongly denied the charge of 'docetism': the flesh was real, and implied real humanity.

Meanwhile, however, others began to see that the old idea that Christ had a human soul could resolve some of the difficulties raised by the Arian argumentation – for the psychological weaknesses could be attributed to this fallible human soul without suggesting that the Logos was fallible. Eustathius of Antioch raised the question why Arians thought it 'important to show that the Christ assumed a body without a soul'. 'Not in appearance and supposition but in very reality God was clothed with a whole man, assuming him perfectly', he said. So the Logos remained impassible and omnipresent; but the Human he assumed, the temple he built for himself, was born, crucified, raised and glorified.

Eustathius is often regarded as passing on an 'Antiochene' or *Word-Man* tradition of christology, which was earlier represented by Paul of Samosata, and later in a more developed form came into conflict with the 'Alexandrian' or *Word-Flesh* tradition represented by Athanasius and his successors. But there are good reasons for thinking that the Arian controversy itself stimulated this development – in fact, created two different responses which eventually produced the two contrasting christologies soon to be at loggerheads.

The affirmation of a human soul in the Christ was not the crucial divide. For the same basic move of attributing psychological weaknesses to the presence of a human soul in the Christ was also made within the Alexandrian tradition around the same date, by Didymus the Blind. Didymus was a quiet scholar in the Origenist tradition who largely avoided the controversies of the fourth century, but he lived all through them as Athanasius' contemporary. Origen had affirmed a human soul in the Christ, but the soul in his schema had a rather different function. It provided the 'metaphysical link' between the Logos and humanity, making the incarnation possible.

* R. P. C. Hanson, *The Search for the Christian Doctrine of God*, T. & T. Clark 1988, p. 448.

It is probable that Didymus picked this up from Origen, but like Eustathius he made use of the idea for a different purpose, namely to turn aside the thrust of Arius' argument that Jesus' human weaknesses implied the creatureliness of the Logos.

Athanasius probably never saw the point. However, possibly before the end of his life, controversy arose about the teaching of a friend of his, Apollinaris of Laodicea, and it may be that he did then accept the necessity of recognizing the presence of a human soul and mind in Christ. However, the text in question may be directed against Arianism, and in any case does not specify 'human'. Athanasius may still have interpreted the phrase, 'not a body without a soul nor without sense or intelligence', as meaning that these life-giving and reason-giving features were provided by the Logos. That is certainly what Apollinaris meant when he used the same expressions, and the basic shape of Athanasius' thinking about the person of Christ appears to have remained unchanged.

The issue about the soul was pressed by Apollinaris' reaction against the kind of development Eustathius and others had made. He probably saw it as a threat to what he took to be Athanasius' principal anti-Arian thrust. For him the Revealer had to be 'God enfleshed' rather than an inspired man. Furthermore, his fundamental assumption seems to have been that every mind is 'self-directing' and it was impossible for two such entities to exist in one person: the Logos and a human soul, or mind, would inevitably be in conflict. What was needed to save humanity was an 'unchangeable mind' which could not fail through temptation and weakness. So 'if Man is composed of three and the Lord is Man, the Lord is of three, spirit, soul and body', but he is 'heavenly Man and living Spirit'.

Understanding Apollinaris' position has been complicated by an apparent conflict in the evidence concerning his understanding of how a human being is constituted: was he 'dichotomist' or 'trichotomist'? In other words, did he believe a person was made up of body+soul, the Logos replacing the soul in Christ, or of body+soul+spirit, the Logos being the 'spirit' in Christ? (In the latter case, the soul would be the natural principle of life, shared with other living creatures.) In fact the debate does not seem to matter in the end, because the issue concerns the 'directing principle' in the person. Apollinaris' terminology is vague rather than precise, and seems largely drawn from the Pauline epistles. His opponents were clear that the consequences of his view were that the whole human being was not assumed and therefore not healed – the mind needed salvation as much as the flesh, they declared. But this seems to have been a new realization provoked by Apollinaris' explicit denials. Like everyone else before this controversy, Athanasius did not seem to discern this need.

Apollinaris' opponents were also concerned about another aspect of his teaching, and this too seems to be rooted in Athanasius' thinking. Athanasius had understood salvation in terms of *theopoiēsis*, deification or divinization: Apollinaris taught that the flesh was assumed into heaven, and also, it seems, that the Logos' flesh pre-existed in heaven. He was the 'Man from heaven', as Paul said. It is not easy to see exactly what he meant, but his opponents certainly expended much energy refuting the idea that the flesh of Christ was eternal.

What lies behind this may be an objection on Apollinaris' part to the Trinity becoming 'four' by the assumption of the flesh, but it seems more likely to relate to his endeavour to give a satisfactory account of the union of the divine Logos with human flesh. The old idea of mediation was no longer viable in the post-Arian situation. Apollinaris reinterprets mediation in terms of the 'mean' between two: the mean between a horse and a donkey is a mule, between white and black is grey, between winter and summer is spring. The mean between God and Man is Christ. Unfortunately this meant a 'mixture' involving dillution of the Godhead and truncation of the Humanity, and there was a strong reaction against this way of approaching the problem. Apollinaris, however, was far from chary of this language. The virgin birth was important for him precisely because it produced a biological freak.

This stress on 'mixture' means that the idea of 'eternal enflesh-ment' is by no means foreign to Apollinaris' approach to the christol-ogical problem. The flesh was 'united in substance (*ousia*)' with God, and so 'his flesh gives us life'. Christ is, and must always have been, a compound unity, an organic union composing a unique mediator. In the end this claim was resisted with more fervour than the denial of the presence of a 'soul' in Christ. The Antiochenes always suspected the Alexandrians of meaning 'mixture' when they spoke of 'hypostatic' or 'natural' union, and it did not matter how often the Alexandrians repeated the anti-Apollinarian refrain that he was united with a body which was 'not without soul and mind', they could never allay their opponents' suspicions that they were Apollinarian.

Contemporary with Apollinaris was Diodore of Tarsus, who is credited with the development, indeed more recently the initiation, of the Antiochene tradition. Diodore may have provoked Apollinaris' views; certainly Apollinaris provoked Diodore! But there is some difficulty in seeing this conflict as the precursor of the later conflict between the two schools. Diodore seems to have been close to Athanasius in attributing human weaknesses to the 'flesh' of Christ, and he never used Theodore's formula, 'the Man assumed' (see below). Nevertheless, he did refuse to make the Logos the direct subject of the incarnate experiences, and this became characteristic of the Antiochene position. 'The one who is the seed of David', or 'the one born of Mary' was the one who suffered, died and was raised, not the Logos. For the Logos is impassible, immortal and unchangeable. He was not 'born' nor was he 'mixed' with flesh – he could not be without compromising his nature. The 'likeness of the Father' must be distinguished from the 'likeness of a servant'. Hence his opponents accused him of teaching 'Two Sons'.

Diodore's confrontation with Apollinaris' ideas may not have exactly been the precursor of the conflict to come, yet in the ensuing conflict the two sides could never quite get rid of the prejudices inherited from this period. To the Alexandrians, the Antiochenes taught 'Two Sons'; to the Antiochenes, the Alexandrians taught an Apollinarian 'mixture'. The ultimate legacy of this mutual suspicion was lasting division in the Eastern church. Branded as 'Nestorians', exiles in Persia preserved the Antiochene tradition and eventually it spread throughout Asia, reaching even China and India. Their survivors were found in Iran in this century. And branded as 'Monophysites', the Coptic and Syrian Jacobite churches have survived the centuries of Islamic rule out of communion with the Orthodox. Ecumenical interest is at last beginning to bring their isolation to an end.

It is difficult to be sure exactly what Diodore taught and how he got there because of the fragmentary nature of the evidence. This is true also of Theodore of Mopsuestia. Both came to be regarded as the original 'Nestorians', and with their condemnation, only damning excerpts were preserved. Theodore, however, remained highly revered as 'The Interpreter' in the Syriac-speaking churches, especially the Nestorian groups in Persia. Some of Theodore's work has therefore been rediscovered in Syriac translation. Unfortunately the really crucial work *On the Incarnation* was lost in the First World War before it was published. So the incriminating fragments torn out of context remain our principal source of information. They can be assessed, however, in the light of other material such as his *Catechetical Homilies*.

Theodore regards as utterly foolish those who think that there is a natural kinship between God and humanity. There is a great chasm between the eternal and the contingent. But the very transcendence of God implies immanence, since the infinite must be everywhere. This universality and eternity belong also to the Logos, for he is 'of one substance' with the Father. Now since he is omnipresent, it is by a special act of favour that he becomes particularly present, as he is by grace in apostles and in the elect. In the incarnation, by habit of will or by special favour, the God-Logos united to himself the 'Man Assumed'. His changelessness meant he could not 'become flesh' except metaphorically. Rather he assumed humanity in its fullness.

For Theodore, salvation depended upon both God and humanity playing their appropriate part: an act of God's creative grace was necessary to restore and heal the fallen creature, and since the will was the seat of sin, humanity had to achieve perfection by exercising that will in obedience to God. This double process uniquely took place in the incarnation of the Logos in Jesus Christ. He was therefore fully divine and fully human. Theodore did not like the language of 'Two Sons', but he did attribute birth, action, suffering, etc. to the Humanity, asserting that it was improper to attribute them to Divinity except indirectly through his gracious uniting of himself with the 'Man Assumed'. Few have been confident that his account of the union was satisfactory. We seem to have a 'schizophrenic' Saviour. This may not be entirely fair to Theodore's thinking, but once the issues came into the open through conflict between Cyril and Nestorius, it became hard to defend his position.

Alexandria had never been happy about the position of the upstart see of Constantinople, and certainly there were 'non-theological factors' in the major christological controversy that dominates the early fifth century. Cyril's uncle, Theophilus, had succeeded in ousting John Chrysostom, the most famous preacher of the early church, and the nephew learned from his tactics. Constantinople had influence because it was the 'New Rome', the new Eastern capital, whose churches had been established by Constantine, and whose bishop had the ear of the emperor. But it was not an ancient, apostolically founded see, as Alexandria claimed to be, and attempts to increase the authority and territorial jurisdiction of Constantinople were deeply resented. Like Chrysostom, Nestorius had a reputation for eloquence and was brought from Antioch to become the new bishop of Constantinople in 427. Quickly he achieved a reputation for being a 'firebrand', hot against heretics. He was young and energetic, and also naive enough to play into Cyril's hands. But that does not necessarily mean that the controversy was about matters of no substance.

Was it then merely a matter of terminology? Was there deliberate perversity or inevitable misunderstanding because of the language used, when really the two sides were not far apart? This has often been suggested, especially since Cyril did reach a Formulary of Reunion with John of Antioch once Nestorius was out of the way. However, there were real differences of theological interest and emphasis, despite these other factors. Maybe the conflict was unfortunate and unnecessary, and reasoned debate would have brought more clarity than the dust of battle, but it was not about nothing, as some have tried to suggest.

Exactly how the controversy arose is not clear since several different accounts have come down to us. What seems to have happened is that two disputing groups appealed to Nestorius to settle their quarrel: should Mary be called 'Theotokos' (that is, Mother of God) or 'Anthropotokos' (Mother of Man), the latter being preferred on the grounds that it was improper to call her Mother of God since God cannot be born? Years later, assuming the authenticity of the Nestorian Apology discovered early this century under the title *The Bazaar of Heracleides* and preserved in Syriac, Nestorius claimed that he suggested the appropriate title was 'Christotokos', and this was accepted by both sides – all would have been well if there had been no outside interference. Nevertheless, there are extant sermons of Nestorius which appear to exclude the term 'Theotokos' altogether, and Cyril clearly thought he was a determined critic of the term. Yet in the letters written during the controversy, Nestorius allows that it may be tolerated and to Cyril he confessed he had nothing against it 'only do not make the Virgin a goddess'. Cyril certainly seems to have exploited somewhat unfairly a situation in which Nestorius may not have been altogether diplomatic, at any rate to begin with.

The correspondence between Cyril and Nestorius has been preserved among the papers of the Ecumenical Councils (*Acta Conciliorum Oecumenicorum*) which were collected from the fifth century on, and these letters not only tell us much about the position argued on each side but also reveal the activities of spies and counter-spies employed by the patriarchs to keep each other posted of developments. That Nestorius had challenged the use of the title 'Theotokos' for the Holy Virgin gave Cyril an excuse to write to the monks of Egypt warning them of false teachings. This was alerting the troops for the coming battle. The target was clearly Nestorius' christological doctrine, and Nestorius was naturally upset. Cyril wrote to Nestorius expressing surprise that he had not considered his own position, since he had raised the issue and caused upset in the first place. Even the Pope was getting concerned about what was going on in Constantinople (though guess who had alerted him to the situation – Cyril, of course!). Some had almost reached the point of holding back from confessing that Christ was God and proposing instead he was a tool of the divinity or a 'God-bearing man', Cyril demanded that Nestorius call the Holy Virgin 'Theotokos' for the sake of peace. Nestorius tried to play it cool, but his brief reply settled nothing.

A few months later, Cyril wrote again, spelling out the christological issues more fully. Here his starting-point is the Nicene Creed, and his fundamental objection to the position Nestorius adopts is that its consequence is the division of the clauses of the creed between the Divinity and the Humanity. Cyril insists that the only-begotten Son of God is the subject of all the credal affirmations: he, himself, was incarnate, lived as man, suffered, rose and ascended.

The Logos united with himself, in his own being or *hypostasis*, flesh animated with a rational soul, and became man. (Note how Cyril made sure he guarded himself against the Apollinarian charge.) One must affirm the mystery that the Logos, even though impassible, suffered on the cross in his own body. So also he was born of a woman according to the flesh, despite that not being the beginning of his existence. Scripture says not that he united himself to a man's person, but that he became flesh. Accordingly there is no objection to calling the Virgin 'Theotokos'. For Cyril the creed demands the involvement of the Logos in the whole incarnational process, even though the manner of his uniting himself with the flesh is 'ineffable and inconceivable'.

Nestorius this time replied with force, retorting that the Nicene Fathers did not teach that the consubstantial Godhead was passible or that the one co-eternal with God had been begotten. The very phrase 'one Lord Jesus Christ, his only-begotten Son' showed how the Fathers had carefully laid side by side the names belonging to each nature so that the one Lord is not divided, while at the same time the natures are not in danger of confusion because of the singleness of the Sonship. The key passages of scripture under discussion, such as Phil. 2.5ff., follow the same pattern, according to Nestorius. When the name Christ is used, this is quite deliberate: it refers to the single *prosōpon* (face, person) of passible and impassible nature – for Christ can be called both impassible and subject to passion, being impassible in his Godhead and subject to passion in his body.

So the body is the 'Temple' of the Godhead, because the Godhead made it its own by a precise divine 'conjunction', and birth, suffering, etc. should be attributed to the Humanity not the Logos. To such a statement Cyril was bound to react badly. His next letter, sent from a Synod of Egyptian bishops, was an abrupt demand that Nestorius submit, with Twelve Anathemas appended. Meanwhile Cyril had kept the Pope primed, and a Synod in Rome earlier in the year (430) had issued a demand that Nestorius recant and confess the same faith as Rome and Alexandria – if he did not do so within ten days of receiving the letter he would be excommunicated. The ultimatum was forestalled by an imperial summons to a General Council in the following year. By that time the East had split into two hostile camps. The 'Oriental' bishops led by John of Antioch were deeply offended by the Twelve Anathemas, and strong pamphlets were quickly issued by Andrew of Samosata and Theodoret of Cyrus, to which Cyril wrote a number of replies justifying them. The Council was bound to be a damaging and disastrous occasion, and it certainly was!

The Council was called for Pentecost at Ephesus. Cyril arrived in good time, accompanied by a large delegation of bishops, with priests and monks to act as supporters around the ring. Nestorius was already there, but the Orientals were delayed. The local bishop was hostile to Nestorius, and facilitated Cyril's move, which was to get the Council started – it was already late. The Council required Nestorius' attendence to answer charges, but Nestorius knew it was packed against him and refused to recognize its authority. The Council proceeded to condemn him, and Cyril sent off a report of the proceedings to the Emperor.

The Orientals eventually arrived and immediately convoked their own Council, agreed a credal statement and excommunicated Cyril. They too sent reports to the Emperor. Finally the papal legates arrived, a month late, and following instructions reported to Cyril. They gave the Pope's approval to what he had done, and so the Council came to be recognized as the Third Ecumenical Council. John of Antioch's proceedings were solemnly set aside. The two bodies never conferred, and when the Emperor's representative arrived he was entirely unable to sort out the situation. Delegations from each side lobbied the court, and the Emperor summoned formal representatives to Constantinople – all to no avail. The Council was dissolved. Meanwhile, however, a successor to Nestorius had been consecrated, and his deposition confirmed. That being the case, Cyril was more disposed to respond positively when John of Antioch opened up peace negotiations. By 433 he had accepted a credal statement John sent, not as replacing the Nicene Creed, but as fulfilling its meaning. After a good deal of pressure, the majority on both sides accepted the Formulary of Reunion, and reluctantly even Theodoret abandoned Nestorius' cause. But the issues were not yet settled – just relatively quiescent for ten years while John of Antioch and Cyril of Alexandria were still alive.

By 447 Theodoret found himself obliged to write against those whose teaching suggested the absorption of the humanity into the one nature of the divinity. The new bishop of Antioch, Domnus, supported him by writing to the Emperor accusing one Eutyches of Apollinarianism. Eutyches was the leader of a community of monks in Constantinople with powerful friends at court, and Domnus' letter triggered a rescript condemning again the writings of Nestorius, and initiating action against those sympathetic to such views. The new bishop of Alexandria, Dioscorus, succeeded in deposing Irenaeus, an old friend of Nestorius, and getting Theodoret confined to his diocese.

Meanwhile, however, the bishop of Constantinople, Flavian, found himself obliged to call Eutyches before a local Synod, and succeeded in getting him excommunicated. Eutyches immediately appealed to the bishops of Rome, Alexandria and elsewhere. World-wide conflict between the two sides became inevitable again. This time, however, Rome's weight was placed on the other side. For Pope Leo could not accept the extreme position adopted by Eutyches. According to Eutyches, Christ took human nature from the Virgin, but that humanity was not consubstantial with ours and was taken up into the one nature of the Incarnate Word. It was not Apollinarianism, but like Apollinarianism it showed up some of the potential implications of an extreme Alexandrian position. For the West there was one nature before the incarnation, namely that of the pre-existent Son, and after their union in the incarnation, two natures united in Christ. Even after Chalcedon the Alexandrian tradition would continue to affirm that there were two natures before the union, and one after (hence the label 'Monophysite').

Dioscorus of Alexandria, not surprisingly, put his weight behind Eutyches and the situation in the East was such that Flavian was forced on to the defensive and had to submit a profession of faith to the Emperor, who meanwhile had resolved on another Council to meet at Ephesus in 449 with Dioscorus as president. The Pope excused himself. Italy was in confusion: since the sack of Rome by Alaric the Goth in 410 there had been no lasting security from the barbarians. But he did write to Flavian, a document traditionally known as the Tome of Leo, an exposition of Western christology which would eventually become authoritative among the papers endorsed at the Council of Chalcedon. But for the present it would have little effect. The Council was carefully set up to favour Alexandria and isolate Domnus of Antioch. The most significant Antiochene theologian, Theodoret, was confined to his remote Syrian see by government order. The papal legates were given places of honour, but never allowed to read out Leo's Tome, or express support for Flavian. Amidst some confusion, the rehabilitation of Eutyches and the deposition of Flavian was skilfully engineered. It was Leo, the Pope, who called it the 'Robber Synod' when reports reached him, and summoned a synod at Rome which annulled the proceedings. But the Emperor Theodosius gave his approval to the Council and its actions and nothing effective could be done until he died. That event occasioned a complete change of government policy. A new Council was called.

The Council of Chalcedon in 451 produced a christological Definition which has remained authoritative for all Western churches, Roman Catholic and Reformed, and for the Orthodox churches of the East. It did not in the end heal the Eastern divisions, though the final rupture between Chalcedonian and non-Chalcedonian churches took a century or more. As at Nicaea, the attempt to unite around a definition of faith was immediately problematic, and this time the consequences were long-term. From a Western perspective, this has often not been appreciated. It inevitably provokes reflection on the ambiguity of the search for uniformity of belief. It has had destructive consequences all along. Nor has it prevented the repeated resurfacing of the same issues between or within denominations. There is an uncanny resemblance between these debates and those that have taken place in modern times, even though the precise issues are different and the controversies are couched in different terms. Much popular Christianity is effectively Arian or Eutychian rather than Chalcedonian, and most attempts to understand christology veer towards one side or other of this ancient struggle.

So sometimes the Chalcedonian Definition is seen as simply setting the parameters within which the christological search is to be conducted, the boundaries outside which it is dangerous to stray. The Definition is seen as a political compromise which does not present any coherent christology, rather a paradox. This leaves it open to challenge, and such challenges often go further than the charge of incoherence, suggesting that the problems arise from 'outdated substance language'. People look for more 'dynamic' categories within which to grapple with the issues, or suggest that we should start all over again and reject the formulations agreed in a completely different cultural and philosophical setting. Given this situation, it is important to appreciate the implicit agenda and its perennial character, as well as attempting to do justice to the doctrinal achievement of the Council.

Let us begin by examining the Definition arrived at by the Council. The first aim was unity and peace in the church. So everyone agreed to endorse the Creed of the 318 (that is, the bishops who met at Nicaea in 325) and the Creed of the 150 (namely the Council that met at Constantinople in 381). These embody what is necessary for godliness and the teaching is complete. They should remain inviolate. In other words, there was to be no new creed. But because of the more recent controversies, it also accepted the second letter of Cyril to Nestorius and the Orientals as in keeping with the creeds, along with the Tome of Leo to Flavian. It is explicitly stated that this is to exclude the errors of Nestorius and Eutyches. Explanation is added:

> For the synod is opposed to those who presume to rend asunder the mystery of the incarnation into a double Sonship, and it deposes from the priesthood those who dare to say that the Godhead of the Only-begotten is passible; and it withstands those who imagine a mixing or confusion of the two natures of Christ; and it drives away those who erroneously teach that the form of a servant which he took from us was of heavenly or some other substance; and it anathematizes those who feign that the Lord had two natures before the union, but that these were fashioned into one after the union.

The Council's targets are evident, and insofar as these targets represented extreme positions which for the most part each side would disavow anyway, the compromise was straightforward.

But the agreed statement went on to try and say something positive:

> Wherefore, following the holy Fathers, we all with one voice confess our Lord Jesus Christ one and the same Son, the same

perfect in Godhead, the same perfect in manhood, truly God and truly man, the same consisting of a reasonable soul and a body, of one substance with the Father as touching the Godhead, the same of one substance with us as touching the manhood, 'like us in all things apart from sin'; begotten of the Father before the ages as touching the Godhead, the same in the last days, for us and for our salvation, born from the Virgin Mary, the Theotokos, as touching the manhood, one and the same Christ, Son, Lord, Only-begotten, to be acknowledged in two natures, without confusion, without change, without division, without separation; the distinction of natures being in no way abolished because of the union, but rather the characteristic property of each nature being preserved and concurring into one person and one subsistence (*hypostasis*), not as if Christ were parted or divided into two persons, but one and the same Son and only-begotten God, Word, Lord, Jesus Christ; even as the prophets from the beginning spoke concerning him, and our Lord Jesus Christ instructed us, and the Creed of the Fathers has handed down to us.

The purpose was clearly to affirm the unity of the one Lord Jesus Christ, the principal concern of Cyril and his successors, while avoiding the 'mixture' so deeply abhorrent to the Antiochenes. But was it merely a compromise, and how successful was it?

The phrase which became the focus of contention was 'in two natures'; the anti-Chalcedonians wanted to amend it to 'out of two natures'. It is easy to laugh at the slight difference between the Greek prepositions *en* and *ek*, just as it was to mock the fight over an 'iota' when disagreement over *homoousios* and *homoiousios* was at issue in the previous century. But the account so far should have alerted us to the ramifications of that apparently slight difference. The affirmation that two natures persist after the union was vital to the Antiochenes and assumed by the West, but it was precisely this that the Alexandrians distrusted as 'dividing the Christ'. The alternative touched the heart of Antiochene suspicions: if you spoke of two natures prior to the union but not after, it suggested a pre-existent humanity and a subsequent 'mixture'. As a compromise it was ultimately doomed to fail.

Despite that, it is clearly a carefully balanced attempt at compromise, giving to each side in turn, and setting up markers against the extreme of each side. Is that all it is? I suggest not, nor do I think that it should be lightly set aside as being straight paradox or culturally limited, bound to an ancient set of philosophical terms and problems. Why not?

In the first place, the basic question was how can one thing be two things at once. Whatever terms that question is expressed in, it remains a natural question, and a persistent challenge to the rational expression of Christian claims. When the question concerns a complex being such as a person or persons rather than a kind of chemistry such as the union of wine and water (an analogy that figured much in the ancient discussions), the matter is even more problematic. The question, 'How can Jesus be God and human at the same time?' is a perennial issue unless it is resolved by popular simplicities like 'Jesus is divine' or 'Christ is unique', implying he is not truly human, and often not truly God but some kind of derivative supernatural Son – indeed, Arianism all over again! That it is really *God* who is revealed and at work in Jesus is one fundamental of the Christian tradition which Chalcedon sought to preserve, and that Jesus was truly human, and therefore able to relate to us and ultimately save us is the other fundamental at issue.

In the second place, the problems arise from the difficulty of understanding the divine nature from the perspective of human creaturely existence. We forget at our peril the ancient struggle with anthropomorphism and idolatry, conceiving of God in personal terms limited by human analogies. The transcendence of the divine was at the heart of the Antiochene thinking, and much loose talk about God suffering should be required to grapple with their concerns. God is 'other' than his creatures. Yet this perception has to be in dialectical relationship with the affirmation that humanity was made in God's image, and he intended sufficient kinship for relationship to be possible. The Antiochenes, I suggest, were grappling with this problem, and seeing in Christ the realization of the perfect union between God and humanity originally intended but shattered by sin. Their inability to encompass this intention through the limitations of human conceptuality, or to persuade their opponents that their attempts to express it in human language were appropriate, is symptomatic of the nature of the problem. The apparent paradox of Chalcedon has the important function of keeping all this in focus. No simple and satisfactory definition within human terms will ever be adequate to the mystery, but that does not absolve us from the necessity of struggling with it, if only to ensure that simplistic and inadequate accounts are seen to be as inappropriate as they are.

And that means that Chalcedon is more than paradox and more than mere parameters. It points in positive directions while standing against the mistaken notion that the problem is like chemistry. It is the very nature of the divine, its unlikeness to anything we know in the created order, which makes possible its union with other being in a way that is not possible for two created beings. Furthermore, the very 'fact' of Christ is a challenge to human assumptions and expectations of the divine, such as the exercise of divine power . . . And here the Alexandrian concern becomes fundamental: it really was the divine Logos who experienced the limitations of human life, and suffered and died, despite the impossibility of our understanding how the principle of life could die, an aspect even more problematic than the debated issue how the impassible could suffer.

6

For Us and for Our Salvation

A superficial reading of the controversies we have been outlining might suggest that they were about notional or even verbal matters which have little relevance in a different cultural and intellectual world. Another less than profound observation exaggerates concern in this period with the doctrines of the Trinity and christology at the expense of the doctrine of salvation. For in fact the controversies which produced the doctrines which reached formal definition were often fired by concern that the gospel of salvation be safeguarded. At the heart of the life of the church was the belief that salvation was being realized, and at the heart of early Christian theology was a sense of the sacramental and spiritual reality of that salvation. Like the Bible, doctrines served the purpose of articulating the saving Word.

More than anything else, recent scholarship has been reclaiming this perspective, and it has already affected the account we have given in previous chapters. The Arian controversy and the Nestorian controversy have been seen as battles for particular views of salvation, just as the controversy with Gnosticism had been. The belief that the sacraments provided the 'medicine of immortality' seems to have fuelled not just the troubles Cyprian found himself in, but also the desire of the Alexandrians to uphold the union of the flesh with the divine, for it was through assimilating the flesh of Christ in the sacrament that *theopoiēsis* (divinization) was effected. Besides this, the more one goes into the subject the more one finds that despite the concentration on these controversies in books on the history of the early church or the formation of doctrine, it is a travesty to suggest that these things constitute the main interest of the vast literature that has come down to us. Much of that literature is preaching material, exposition of the Bible, collections of canonical rules or ethical, pastoral or spiritual treatises, far removed from the struggles we have been exploring, and indicative of the on-going life of the church behind it all.

There was a close relationship between doctrine and life, including liturgy, spirituality, ethics and lifestyle. So as we explore ideas about salvation, we shall inevitably go over ground already covered in earlier chapters. In the past, ideas about salvation in the early church have been explored retrospectively, with an eye not so much on their own cultural and theological context as on anticipations of later theories, particularly those formulated in the Middle Ages. This has had distorting effects which we will try to rectify. What we will find is a wide range of themes, often expressed through imagery and symbol, and the integration of these thematic and symbolic approaches in several different 'theories' by some of the thinkers of the early church, theories in fact embedded in their christology.

Irenaeus, we remember, was a particularly significant doctrinal pioneer in a number of areas, though regarding himself as the arch-conservative. At one point in his writings he says:

> The Lord through his passion destroyed death, brought error to an end, abolished corruption, banished ignorance, manifested life, declared truth, and bestowed incorruption (*Adversus Haereses* II.20.2).

In that sentence he encompassed the principal themes found in the early texts concerning salvation in Christ, who was, as scripture taught, the Way, the Truth and the Life. So for the Apostolic Fathers and Apologists of the second century, he revealed the right *way* of life, fulfilling the highest moral ideals of humanity and so surpassing the philosophers, who in this period were largely preoccupied with ethical issues. It was widely held that virtue was knowledge – for surely anyone who knew what was truly good would do it. Thus, the Saviour brought error to an end and banished ignorance. He also brought knowledge of *truth*, the truth about God being embodied in him – so he was the true revelation desired by gnostic or mystical seekers, as well as the true goal of philosophy and the end of idolatry and false religion. He was also the bringer of *life* and immortality: he bestowed incorruption and through his passion destroyed death. Through death came life: except a grain of wheat fall into the earth and die it does not bear fruit. Logos-theology (see Chapter 3) was an excellent 'theory' embracing these claims: for the Logos was conceived as the principle of life as well as the rationality and goodness which constituted the cosmic order. In Jesus this Logos became flesh and dwelt among us, demonstrating the Way, revealing the Truth and imparting Life.

These themes Irenaeus picked up, and summed up in some telling phrases:

> Because of his measureless love, he became what we are in order to enable us to become what he is (*Adv. Haer.* V.praef.).

> The Logos became human, that humanity united with the Logos and receiving his adoption, might become the Son of God (*Adv. Haer.* III.19).

Now, as we saw earlier, Irenaeus was struggling with the Gnostics who denied the goodness of creation. For them salvation was escape from this alien material universe to the spiritual world to which the fragmented sparks of the divine really belonged. Against this Irenaeus proposed a doctrine of salvation as re-creation, for what was necessary was the restoration of God's original creative intention. Irenaeus had a 'theory' of salvation, though it is quite different from any of the so-called atonement theories which developed later. The 'recapitulation' idea, as well as the Logos-theology he inherited, allowed him to integrate the various themes we noted to start with. Adam had the chance to grow to moral and spiritual maturity, but made the wrong choice; Christ became what we are, and as a 'second Adam' went over the ground again:

> . . . the sin of the first-created was amended by the chastisement of the first-begotten. . . .Therefore he renews all things in himself, uniting humanity to the Spirit (*Adv. Haer.* V.19–21).

Irenaeus still thinks in terms of an End of the world in which this restoration will be consummated, and resists the 'otherworldly' ideas of the gnostics. Necessarily this implies the resurrection of the body, the restoration of the whole person by the creative power of God, and not some inherent immortality of the soul as Platonists assumed (but not others in general). The credal doctrine of the resurrection of the flesh affirms that the bodily existence of humanity is to be healed and restored along with its moral and spiritual being, and the eucharist, for Irenaeus a joyful sacrifice of thanksgiving offering back to God the good things of this creation, then becomes spiritual food, or as Ignatius put it, a kind of 'drug' or 'medicine' that imparts immortality to those who participate.

The background to these ideas is of course the hope of Jewish Apocalyptic for a new heaven and a new earth to arise from the ashes of the old, but for Irenaeus this hope is anticipated through participation in the Body of Christ: he became what we are so that we might become what he is. Salvation could be described as a very 'physical' thing, almost accomplished by the simple fact of the incarnation, but also involving the conquest of evil (the devil hovers in the background for all the writers of the early church, and sometimes takes centre stage), as well as cleansing and forgiveness, revelation and example, empowering, healing and restoring. So various traditional themes are integrated into a picture sharply opposed to the Gnostic view, and the appropriation of the salvation achieved by Christ is closely linked with the sacraments as well as ethics and lifestyle.

Irenaeus, then, integrated a number of traditional themes. As well as these themes we find many symbols and images used by preachers of the early centuries to convey what Christ meant and what he accomplished on behalf of humanity. The symbols and images were drawn from the scriptures. Thus Melito of Sardis in the mid-second century had developed an elaborate parallel, which would become traditional in Easter sermons, between Christian salvation and the story of Passover and Exodus. (There were precedents in the New Testament: Paul said, 'Christ our Passover is sacrificed for us' (I Cor. 5.7); and John's gospel tells the story of the Passion in such a way as to draw out the same parallel.) Melito graphically describes the escape from Egypt, and the way the people of God were saved by the blood of the Lamb; he then describes the fall of Adam and the enslavement of humanity to the devil (as the Israelites were slaves to Pharaoh), and how the human race was rescued by the blood of Christ. He also shows how this was prefigured in other stories, such as the death of Abel, the binding of Isaac, the selling of Joseph, the exposure of Moses and the persecution of David. This process of understanding one story in terms of another is called 'typology', and Irenaeus' 'recapitulation' view is similarly typological, drawing parallels and contrasts between the story of Adam and Christ. Such 'types', as well as texts understood as prophetic predictions by unpacking the riddles of their symbolic language, provided the images and symbols through which salvation was articulated and grasped.

The process of searching scripture for such images, types and symbols led to the development of many 'names' or titles used for Christ as Saviour. That lists of these names became traditional in Christian preaching can be seen in a number of texts from different periods, and a scholar like Origen is indebted to this tradition in expounding the Name of Christ in his *Commentary on John*. He wants to distinguish between names which express what the Logos is in himself and those which he is only for us, but for our purposes the point of interest lies in the way each title is expounded in relation to our salvation and justified by quotation of texts drawn from both Old and New Testaments.

The list includes: Wisdom, Word, Life, Truth, Son of God, Righteousness, Saviour, Propitiation, Light of the World, First-born of the Dead, Good Shepherd, Physician, Healer, Redemption, Resurrection and Life, Way, Truth and Life, Door, Messiah, Christ, Lord, King, Vine, Bread of Life, First, Last, the Living One, Alpha and Omega – First and Last, Beginning and End, Lion of Judah, Jacob/Israel, Shepherd, Rod, Flower, Cornerstone, a Chosen Shaft, Sword, Servant of God, Lamb, Light of the Gentiles, Lamb of God, Paraclete (= Comforter or Advocate), Power of God, Sanctification, High-Priest. Some of the titles express the themes we examined above, others are simply straight christological claims culled in particular from John's gospel or the Book of Revelation, some are drawn from prophetic texts taken to be Messianic, others again are symbols drawn from material in Psalms, and so on. Each is expounded as describing the saving activity of the Logos in relation to humanity.

This might suggest a rather chaotic lack of attention to what salvation is really about, but it seems that there is a 'theory' behind Origen's wealth of imagery. All these titles are important precisely because Christ is a 'multitude of goods'. The fundamental conception with which Origen works is that the oneness of God and the multiplicity of creation is united in the Saviour. He provides the 'linkage' between the Ultimate One and the Many, a classic problem of contemporary Middle Platonist philosophy. Origen's idea of atonement is that the transcendent One God is re-united with his marred creation in what he sometimes called the 'second God'.

This is never entirely spelt out, and as a result interpreters have variously emphasized elements in Origen's thinking and regarded them as most fundamental. Thus, for some, Origen is the intellectual *par excellence*, one for whom revelation and education is the main idea of salvation. For others, the principal thrust of Origen's thought concerns the love of God and his act to save humanity from sin, death and the devil, the devil being overcome when he tried to capture in death the principle of life itself. Yet others have noticed how Origen picks up ideas about atoning sacrifice from the scriptures, and suggests that Christ offered the full, perfect and sufficient sacrifice. Every one of these points is important, but the suggestion here is that they all contribute to a perspective which is not identical with any one of them, namely the re-integration of all things and their restoration to their original perfection, through the union of God and his creation in the Mediator Christ. Given the whole context of Origen's thought (see above Chapter 3), it is not surprising that he generally understood this as a spiritual integration; for the material world was for him an interim arrangement for reformative purposes. So resurrection tended to be 'spiritualized' and understood in terms of the soul's immortality, and we find considerable ambivalence about the flesh in his thinking. Yet once again we can see how ideas of salvation and christological doctrines are closely related. For this atonement to be effected, Christ had to be both One with the Father and a 'multitude of goods' with the creatures.

The conception of Christ as a Mediator, placed on a kind of hierarchical ladder of being, was to be first defended and finally repudiated in the course of the Arian controversy. Yet Athanasius presents an equally multifaceted picture of the Saviour:

Being with him as Wisdom, and as Word seeing the Father, he created the universe, formed it and ordered it; and being the

Power of the Father, he gave all things the strength to come into existence . . . His holy disciples teach that everything was created through him and for him, and that being the good offspring of a good Father and true Son, he is the Power of the Father and his Wisdom and Word, not by participation . . . but he is absolute Wisdom, very Word, and himself the Father's own Power, absolute Light, absolute Truth, absolute Justice, absolute Virtue, and indeed stamp, effulgence and image. In short, he is the supremely perfect issue of the Father, and is alone Son, the express Image of the Father . . . he is the Word and Wisdom of the Father, and at the same time condescends to created beings; to give them knowledge and an idea of the Father, he is absolute Holiness and absolute Life, he is Door, Shepherd and Way, King, Guide and Saviour for all. Life-giver and Light and universal Providence (*Contra Gentes* 46–7).

Again we may discern an underlying 'theory'. Particulars are utterly different from transcendent absolutes or 'ideas', but they can participate in such absolutes and so become 'holy', 'just', 'wise', etc. Such was Plato's basic notion. For Athanasius, the Logos of God cannot be a mediating being, for he constitutes the transcendent Absolute embracing all absolutes, and is therefore truly one with God and on the divine side of a clear line between the Creator and creatures. Particular creatures, however, may participate in the Absolute and so acquire the qualities of holiness, goodness, etc. This depends, however, on the Absolute being different from the participating particulars: the Absolute cannot simply be another instance of each quality.

As we follow Athanasius' exposition in the second volume, his work *On the Incarnation*, we see that (as noted in Chapter 2) salvation is fundamentally understood as re-creation. For at creation humanity was endowed with the Logos, the principle of Reason and Life, and so could participate in the absolutes. But through Adam's disobedience, humanity lost that endowment. So human creatures were drifting back into the nothingness from which they had been created. This put God in a kind of quandary: he could not go back on his word that disobedience would lead to death without losing his integrity, but on the other hand his goodness and love for his creation were threatened by the consequences. So the incarnation of the

Logos was the only possible solution, allowing the re-endowing of humanity with the principle of Reason and Life. So idolatry and ignorance, sin and death were overcome. Particular human beings could participate in the Absolute Sonship of God:

> He became human that we might become divine
> (*De Incarnatione* 54).

For Athanasius salvation is *theopoiēsis* or *huiopoiēsis*, that is 'divinization' or 'filiation' (the making of gods or sons). He did not imagine that those saved became 'god' or 'son' in the same sense as the Saviour is God or Son of God. Those saved are adopted, and so participate in the Absolute Sonship or Godhead that belongs to the Logos. Again we can see the close relationship between such ideas of salvation and the christological debates. For Athanasius only the idea of the Logos or Son being *homoousios* (of the same substance) with the Father could guarantee salvation.

Athanasius' view is often described as 'physical', meaning that the incarnation itself effected salvation. Western critics have suggested that sin is less important to Athanasius than death, and that the incarnation submerges the cruciality of the cross. But this is not altogether true. Death reigns because of sin, and mortality being the consequence, more than mere repentence and forgiveness is required. Furthermore, Athanasius is clear that only by his sacrificial death could Christ rescue humanity from death and sin. As in all the patristic material, the notion of God overcoming the devil and the powers of evil within whose grip humanity languishes, is also present, though Athanasius is clear that ultimate responsibility lies with God, since God alone is the source of all, and it was God's broken decree which caused the problems. He has seen that God's own justice and integrity is under threat because of his mercy and love. It is in these ways that Athanasius integrates the themes and symbols he has inherited, and he came nearest to expounding a systematic 'theory' of atonement. It has some Platonic features, refining Origen's idea of mediation by highlighting the notion of participation of particulars in the Absolute; it has many features similar to the Irenaean picture of the re-creation and restoration of God's creature.

Generally speaking it may be said that Athanasius' approach has formed the approach of Eastern Christianity, allowing mystical and sacramental experience to find theological expression in a view of salvation which emphasizes *theopoiēsis* and focusses more on the incarnation and the resurrection than the sacrificial death of Christ. But as we have seen, the death of Christ was not unimportant, and there were two basic ways in which early theologians attempted to understand it. One was to suggest it was a sacrifice to propitiate God's anger, a motif rooted in pagan assumptions that sacrifice was some sort of bribe to keep the gods sweet, though it was possible to read this perspective into some biblical texts and that was done very effectively by Christian preachers like John Chrysostom. Alongside this, however, and in tension with it was the much more pervasive idea that it was a means of conquering the devil and the powers of evil.

A lively sense of the reality of Satan had been inherited from Jewish Apocalyptic, which clearly had a considerable influence on New Testament and second-century Christianity where it was not Gnostic in tendency. The plight of humanity was attributed to the blandishments of the Tempter, and the world was seen as under the dominion of supernatural evil powers. The notion expressed in Colossians 2.15 that Christ had 'disarmed the cosmic powers and authorities' was related to his death on the cross. From very early on the idea of 'ransom' was understood in terms of God offering the devil a ransom-price in order to free humanity from slavery. Martyrs were seen as engaging in the on-going struggle on the side of Christ, and their mantle was inherited by the monks with the rise of the monastic movement. So as Athanasius (or perhaps some other unknown author) describes in the *Life of Antony*, ascetics went off into the desert, the abode of the demons, to do battle with them, and according to the Long Recension of his work *On the Incarnation*, Christ died suspended on a cross in order to hang in the air and purify it of demonic powers.

But how was this effected? Many do not seem to have needed an explanation, probably understanding it instinctively in terms of an 'aversion' sacrifice, that is a rite or offering to keep away evil spirits. The blood of the Passover lamb kept away the angel of death, and that 'type' was enough. However, some of the Fathers tried to explain. For some, the sin of Adam meant that the devil had rights over humankind, and as a moral Being, God had to respect those rights and do a deal with him. Others saw God's rescue mission as an act of overwhelming love in which the Deceiver was Deceived. Having got humanity in his grip the devil was able to exact the death penalty for sin. Like a fisherman, God offered him a tempting bait, and he went for it, only to find he had tried to swallow one who could not be held in death, because he was both innocent and the very principle of life. So the power of the devil was broken by the resurrection. It is interesting that some of the most sophisticated of the Fathers were prepared to entertain such ideas, people like Origen and Gregory of Nyssa. It seems that their motivation was a strong doctrine of God's love which could not rest comfortably with the other tradition, namely that God's anger had been propitiated by the sacrifice of Christ.

But there were some who found such explanations of how the power of evil was broken quite unacceptable on moral and theological grounds. They anticipated the objections of Anselm in the Middle Ages, and many modern historians of the Doctrine of Atonement who have dismissed such ideas as mythological. Gregory of Nazianzus, for example, thought that the popular notion that the devil received Christ as a ransom-price was outrageous. But how could the offering be made to God? he asked. It was not from slavery to God that humanity needed redemption. Nor does God need or delight in sacrifice. The Father accepted it, he concludes 'because of the economy', by which he seems to mean his 'plan of salvation', the need to sanctify humanity by God's humanity, to overcome the tyrant, and draw us to himself by the mediation of his Son. Gregory, I suggest, was trying to say what Athanasius was feeling after. Despite the fact that most studies of Athanasius have described his view of salvation as 'physical', and Gustaf Aulen treated him as the principal exponent of the idea that Christ was Victor over the powers of evil,* Athanasius, as we have seen, had a sense that since God is the source of all, he must ultimately bear responsibility for the presence of evil in his creation, and so the cross was a kind of 'self-propitiation', reconciling God's integrity with love, mercy with

* Gustav Aulen, *Christus Victor*, SPCK 1934.

justice. Yet this was but one aspect of the whole saving and healing process whereby God re-created his marred creation.

This account of patristic approaches to salvation, though somewhat sketchy, should provide an explanation for the fact that scholars telling the history of the doctrine of atonement have always been able to find anticipations of later doctrines in the patristic material. The classic histories were written at the beginning of this century, and they were shaped by the current conflict between so-called liberals and conservatives both catholic and evangelical. The latter asserted that the traditional doctrine of atonement, as enunciated by Anselm in the Middle Ages and anticipated in the early material, was in terms of 'penal substitution': Christ bore the punishment due to humanity by sacrificing himself on our behalf and so satisfying God's justice and rescuing humanity from his judgment. Summarized like that, it is a confused doctrine deserving of criticism and not in any case representing what Anselm himself taught. The liberals provided criticisms aplenty and suggested that Abelard's view was more appropriate to Christian theology, emphasizing as it did the overwhelming demonstration of God's love on the cross which brings about repentence and so reconciliation. For this they found many anticipations in the Fathers. Neither side could do justice to the patristic statements about conquest of the devil.

It was in response to this rather polarized position that Gustaf Aulen resurrected what he called the 'Classic Theory of Atonement', explaining the tendencies towards dualism in the early church and how central was the notion that in Christ the powers of evil were overcome. But then it was evident that that approach too did not account for much of the material. H. E. W. Turner explored the patristic doctrine of redemption in terms of four basic approaches: the educative, the 'physical', the 'ransom' or conquest motif and the idea of sacrifice. Dillistone pursued many motifs, eschewing the notion of a theory.*

What has been suggested here is that early expressions of a sense of salvation and atonement are almost chaotically varied because

---

* See Gustav Aulen, *Christus Victor*, SPCK 1934; H. E. W. Turner, *The Patristic Doctrine of Redemption*, Mowbray 1952; F. W. Dillistone, *The Christian Understanding of Atonement*, 1968, SCM Press 1984.

they draw on all kinds of imaginative images, symbols, 'types', particularly drawn from the poetry of the Bible approached as prophetic and spiritual in its intent. And yet Christian thinkers integrated this wealth of material into 'systematic theologies' in which the whole of Christian doctrine hung together. Although they differ somewhat from thinker to thinker and century to century, most of these were conceived as a marriage between the earthly and heavenly realms, the material and the spiritual, the divine and the human. To this extent their approach to the theology of the sacraments, their understanding of the biblical texts, their ideas about salvation and their christologies were all likewise a search for uniting Two Natures in One.

Now this discussion, like much of the rest of this book, implies a certain tension in Christian thought between a monistic and a dualistic outlook. In order to clarify our thinking we have to distinguish a variety of types of dualism, some of which had a persistent influence, even though the church defined itself over against other forms. The dualism which most deeply affected the church, particularly the intellectuals, was that of Platonism. We see it in the theology of Origen, and in the Neoplatonic mystical spirituality which influenced the thinking of such as Gregory of Nyssa and Augustine.

Some might say that this was not really dualistic – for Plotinus, the leading Neoplatonist philosopher also rejected gnostic dualism. Platonism, however, had its basic distinction between Being and Becoming, and this was easily related to distinctions between soul and body, the spiritual and the material. This was a mode of thinking that was receptive of ascetic ideals seen as the stripping of the soul of material distractions so as to pursue knowledge of moral and spiritual realities, the eternal rather than the transient. It tended to encourage the spiritualizing of the idea of resurrection, and the definition of matter, like evil, as 'non-being'. So much of early Christian spirituality gives the impression of aiming to rise above material existence, rather as Origen sought to leave the 'literal' meaning of scripture and probe its deeper reference to transcendent realities. Such assumptions, which imply some kind of metaphysical dualism, seem almost unquestioned in many texts, and yet interestingly enough, even in Origen's thought, the material world and the literal meaning appear at times as the sacramental vehicle of spiritual realities.

The legacy of this dualism is evident in later Christian presuppositions about the immortality of the soul and the corruption of the body, yet in this period serious attempts to discuss human nature and destiny embrace this dualism in a unifying vision. As already mentioned in Chapter 2, Nemesius of Emesa (about whom we know little more than his name) towards the end of the fourth century wrote a treatise *On Human Nature*, and using Galen's medical philosophy and ancient discussions about such matters as the relationship between soul and body and the workings of sense perception and emotions, arrived at a picture of humanity as the connecting link between the material and spiritual worlds, as a complex unity of soul and body created that way by the Creator. Gregory of Nyssa linked similar ideas with a vision of humanity as the crown of creation to be restored to the place God intended at the resurrection. Despite his Neoplatonism he did not come up with a picture of disembodied souls in a spiritual heaven, but with an eschatology in which the material is transformed and taken up into a renewed order of creation as God originally intended it to be. If in practice it seemed to both that the choice between the material and the spiritual was crucial, so that the flesh was easily associated with bestial desires and became a downward drag on the soul's ascent, ultimately, as in the sacraments, the good things of this material world and even our human bodies, were to be transformed into spiritual bodies fed by spiritual food. The legacy of Irenaeus and the struggle with the gnostics lived on, despite the pressures against it, and the resurrection of the body was not entirely submerged by the Platonic doctrine of the soul's immortality.

What Christian thinkers rejected from the second century on was the assumption that the dualism of spiritual and material meant two ultimate eternal principles: God – Matter. The duality of material and spiritual was contained within the created order, and the only First Principle was God the transcendent Creator, who brought the created order into being out of nothing. The purpose of God was that the creation be united with him, and yet that union involved the differentiation of creature and Creator. Distinctively Christian mysticism and the doctrine of *theopoiēsis* has never envisaged simple absorption into the divine. The Platonic notion of a natural kinship between the soul and the divine, espoused by Origen, was abandoned at the time of the Arian controversy. Union with the divine came to be seen as a mystical marriage, a uniting of two distinct natures, one of which was contingent, entirely dependent on the other for its very existence, and yet created as a mirror-image of it, as Genesis affirmed. The struggle to enunciate a proper doctrine of incarnation was not unrelated to the refining of an appropriate spirituality.

Despite overlap, this kind of dualism is different from the dualisms *against* which the church defined itself, dualisms like those of the Gnostics in which the material creation and its Creator were seen as alienated from the truly divine and as the source of evil. In the later period the church was confronted by an extreme type of gnostic dualism in Manichaeism. Augustine was for a time a Manichee. This type of dualism acknowledged two eternal principles, Light and Dark, with which Good and Evil were respectively associated. The present world order was the result of their unfortunate confusion, and the children of Light could not hope to improve it: rather they should seek escape to their proper realm. This view produced a radical asceticism, all Manichees practising vegetarianism, and the Elect keeping themselves pure by abstaining from wine, personal possessions, sex and marriage as well as not being able to engage in any production of fresh life, needing a disciple even to prepare their own food. The reason for this was that particles of Light were trapped in the physical and the Elect could not be party to compounding the situation; yet the act of eating could be a kind of sacrament releasing Light from its contamination.

This may be described as an ultimate dualism, even more ultimate than most gnostic systems, for no initial or final unity is envisaged – in fact, the direct opposite. Augustine's conversion from Manichaeism through Neoplatonism was from such an ultimate dualism to a kind of monism. He discovered that evil did not have any real existence, but was the deprivation or absence of good. In an important sense that was a genuine revision of his fundamental metaphysical conceptions, and an indication of the difference between Platonic dualism and Gnostic kinds of dualism. The church rejected Manichaeism on the same grounds as it had earlier rejected Gnosticism: for besides its blasphemous failure to honour the Creator as the all-sufficient all-good only-divine First Cause, the Manichees' view of Jesus was docetic, and their notion of salvation was release from the material.

Yet within the church some ascetics, particularly some extremist groups, were not so far from a total rejection of the material. The bishops of the church found themselves obliged to exclude one such group, the Messalians, and continually preachers had to affirm that the way of discipleship in the world was not inferior to that of the Holy Man who adopted a radical lifestyle of self-denial. A certain 'otherworldliness' has been endemic in Christian idealism through-out most of Christian history. Many in our day suggest that Christian ambivalence about the body lies at the root of unhealthy attitudes to sex, not to mention the tendency to keep women inferior by blaming them in the person of Eve for temptation and sin. Yet the church explicitly defined itself over against such extreme world-denying views, while honouring those who sought to sublimate the material in a life of spirituality – so blurring the issue.

This was possible partly because there was a third kind of dualism which Christianity inherited from Jewish apocalyptic, the rather pessimistic view that in the present evil age, Satan has dominion over the earth, and yet ultimately God is Sovereign and his kingdom will be restored. So now, they thought, there is a cosmic conflict going on, but ultimately God will triumph. This might be called a practical (but not ultimate) dualism.

As we have seen, this kind of outlook was the context of much preaching of Christian salvation. People had a lively sense of the rejection of the world, the flesh and the devil when they were initiated in baptism. They were exorcized, and cast out the demons of their past, the pagan gods they had once worshipped. They took on a new citizenship, and tended to see Rome as Babylon ruled by Satan. They enlisted in a new army, becoming soldiers of Christ, and took the oath of allegiance (*sacramentum*). Martyrs were the great heroes, to be succeeded by the monks and ascetics who led the fight against the powers of evil. Christ had achieved the victory, but all Christian disciples were engaged in the 'mopping-up oper-ation'. They could face death fearlessly because ultimate victory was assured.

This practical dualism was eventually explained as the result of the precosmic Fall of Lucifer. God was acknowledged as Creator and King of the earth, and Lucifer (the Light-bearer) was the highest of his angels. But he attempted to usurp God's throne, betraying

God's trust. So behind the dualism was an ultimate monism which allowed the church to differentiate its position from dualisms of the gnostic type. In theory this was God's world, though not in practice. So this practical dualism allowed hospitality to world-rejecting enthusiasm, and made it difficult to develop a 'this-worldly' lifestyle or ideology.

Eusebius, the historian of the church, did attempt to show how Providence had brought about the unity of the world when Christ came, and was introducing the kingdom of God through Constantine who had made Rome Christ's. Thus he resisted dualistic views of the historical process and rejected Apocalyptic ideas, like the Millenarianism of the (non-Gnostic) second century (the view that there would be a Thousand Year Reign of Christ on earth after the Second Coming, when the prophecies of triumph would be fulfilled). But the increasing compromises with the world that were consequent upon the political changes that came with Constantine fuelled ascetic radicalism, kept rejection of the world alive, and produced potential tensions between the hierarchy and the monastic movement which were contained with some difficulty. The consequent conflict of ideals had a profound personal effect on the lives of many fourth-century figures, like Basil of Caesarea and his friend Gregory, or indeed John Chrysostom.

So Christianity rejected an ultimate dualism, while recognizing that a simple philosophical monism was impossible. It was not just that the doctrine of the Trinity was itself a denial of a simple monism, recognizing as it did a certain uni-complexity in the Being of God himself, but also that God's relationship with the world necessitated a certain recognition of duality, for two basic reasons:

First, if monism is taken too seriously there is no room for anything else to exist but God and everything becomes God in some sense. But if God is Creator, then he has freely chosen to allow things other than himself to exist, and the differentiation of Creator and creature, as we have seen, became an important element in developing Christian thinking. So too did a practical recognition of the difference between material and spiritual reality, though this was transformed by the refusal to accept that the spiritual was inherently divine and eternal – indeed it too was created by God and held in being by God. Creation consisted of a complex material-spiritual reality, and this complex creation was ultimately to be restored to the perfection it had once enjoyed, which consisted in an appropriate union of love with the Creator. Not for nothing was Christian spirituality focussed on the Song of Songs and the notion of the church as the bride of Christ.

Secondly, if monism is taken too seriously, there is no room for a doctrine of salvation, since everything must be of God and therefore perfect. Yet, the world is evidently not perfect, and human beings fall morally short of the glory of God. The basic notion of salvation in the patristic period would appear to be God's act to restore the unity and perfection of the original creation. This involved healing and re-creating, and so also that cleansing and reparation which could alone atone for the sin which had disrupted the relationship. But this salvation could be expressed in highly dualistic terms – for the loss of that perfection could be seen as rebellion resulting in conflict, indeed as enslavement to a rebellious spiritual power. Salvation always implies dealing with that which is not of God, and so implies a practical dualism. Hence the curious tension in early Christian theology between resistance to dualism with the consequent affirmation of one good God who created a good world, and the stress on the need for atonement, for redemption from evil, for choice of the higher spiritual way in preference to material concerns and bestial desires.

But that barely conceals another tension in Christian theology: does salvation come through making such a choice and exercising freewill for good, or is it effected through the grace of God? The logic of salvation through the incarnation was an integration of opposites effected for the whole cosmos, a union of what had become dual, the transformation of the fleshly by healing its corruption, and salvation made real through the sacraments, which were both 'physical' and immaterial. That meant re-creation through the gracious gifts of the Creator. Yet the logic of that could be an 'automatic' salvation, and some have suggested that Athanasius' doctrine implied just that. In fact, however, the apologetic tradition that opposed fate and the ethical tradition that preached moral choice were deeply engrained, and Athanasius' fundamental outlook allowed for choice as to whether one was adopted into Christ or not, whether this 'particular' would participate in this saved humanity rather than that of Adam. In fact Eastern theology managed to hold together in creative tension both the divine saving initiative and human responsibility, and this is particularly evident in the preaching of one like John Chrysostom: only a short-sighted criticism sees his moralism as 'Pelagian'. That very label derives from the fact that the West was less successful.

For Augustine came into a damaging conflict with a British monk called Pelagius over this issue, a conflict which had a lasting legacy and resurfaced at the Reformation. Pelagius arrived in Rome and was horrified at the moral laxity of those who professed to be Christian; he was even more horrified when he found it justified by reference to a prayer used by Augustine: 'Command what you will, and give what you command.' People were so to speak 'waiting on the Lord' instead of making a moral effort. Since perfection is possible, it is obligatory, Pelagius asserted: in his view there could be no excuses like 'It's only human.'

A long debate ensued, though Augustine and Pelagius never met face to face. It covered issues like the meaning of freewill and grace, original sin and predestination. Pelagius' view had deep roots in Christian tradition: God created us with freewill and presents us with a choice, Christ has shown us the way, all we have to do is obey his commands. It was based on a rather simple view of sin as wrong acts, and on the power of the individual to make isolated moral decisions. Logically it left no room for salvation since moral prowess rested on personal endeavour. Yet Pelagius had a clear perception of the goodness and grace of God in providing us with the best environment for moral development. Many people take Pelagius' position for granted without knowing anything about this controversy.

Augustine, however, knew that his conversion had been a 'gift' not a desert. His salvation was the result of God, as it were, taking him in hand. Until he was freed of the tendency to sin which had enslaved him, he had no hope of following Christ. His whole moral being was dependent on God's grace. These instincts were worked out as a doctrine of original sin, inherited from Adam, which meant that all humanity was a 'mass of perdition'; the very sex act which produced the new human being was concupiscence, lustful desire, and infant baptism was practised, according to Augustine, precisely to free the new-born of that incubus and provide a chance for 'freedom' and the possibility of moral choice. Many find such a doctrine deeply offensive, especially as it led logically to predestination: for in the end, Augustine argues, salvation depends not at all upon ourselves but upon God's sovereign decision to save or condemn.

Yet there is something to be said for Augustine's position. The gospel of salvation depends upon the view that humanity is sick and needs healing, that there are structures of evil from which we cannot individually release ourselves by any amount of moral effort. For sin is not simply a matter of individual wrong acts: some of the worst sins are 'social', issuing from environment and corporate loyalties, and these are often not perceived to be sin by the perpetrators (e.g. racism). Furthermore, Augustine's understanding of concupiscence was not limited to sexual desire: he was probing the profound egocentricity we all inherit, the pride which inhibits the possibility of true relationship with God. To that extent Augustine was far nearer to understanding both scripture and tradition, and his perceptions were religiously deeper than the simplistic moralizing of his opponent. The trouble was Augustine seemed to leave no room for any human response or reaction, and so to turn God's sovereignty into dictatorial and arbitrary whim. There is much else in his theology which should have prevented that: for he above all appreciated that God's very Being as Trinity was Love, and love was the motivation for and energy of his creating and saving activity. What Augustine failed to appreciate was that true love allows the other to be, lets the other go, waits for the prodigal's return, while binding up the wounds of the broken-hearted and healing the world's 'gone-wrongness'.

The balance of Christian theology necessitates an on-going but potentially creative struggle with the tension between God's grace and human freewill, between the imperatives of faith and works, between the divine initiative and human responsibility. This is not unrelated to a somewhat parallel struggle with the tension between a doctrine of creation and a doctrine of redemption. For the one implies perfection and the other imperfection, the one implies monism and the other dualism, yet Christian theology has never been able to rest with the choice of one to the exclusion of the other.

Indeed, the early thinkers saw them as closely related: for redemption was the re-creative activity of God consummating the original intention, completing the initial work, uniting in one what remained ever two.

Concluding Reflections

Every group of people seeks self-definition in terms of distinctive characteristics that mark it off from others. Every community is in this sense exclusive, and the history of the church is no different from other human social groupings in this respect. A group coheres around a common interest, or esoteric rites and rules, creating boundaries. Judaism as a national religious community has its marks of membership, circumcision, endogamy and the practice of the Law. The interesting question about Christianity is why, having broken across national and racial divides, its boundaries and defining marks became principally matters of belief rather than behaviour, or some other feature. The intolerant enforcement of conformity and persecution of deviants is not distinctive: communities which gain power tend to exact conformity and oppress those who do not fit accepted rules of normality. But that the test should be in terms of orthodoxy rather than behaviour or tribal solidarity is more unusual, except where ideologies have formed themselves on the Christian pattern. Why did acceptance of a creed or doctrinal basis become essential?

We have traced a story which provides some degree of explanation. Loyalty to the one true God was inherited from Judaism, and very quickly the community had to define its loyalty in response to accounts of the way the world is which challenged the sovereignty, the goodness and the unity of the Creator. So the issue of truth became paramount, more passionately so than for the philosophers whose urbane disagreements had long since occasioned criticism and fostered a drift into a kind of relativism and scepticism. The sects and schools were called *haereses*, choices or options, and there was a feeling it made little difference which you chose. Justin came to feel differently, and it is in his work that we can see a renewed passion for the truth as he espouses Christianity as the fulfilment of the philosophical quest. Soon Christians regarded the existence of *haereses* or variant views of truth as fundamentally wrong, damaging the unity perceived to lie at the heart of things. Heresy became a problem, and heretics had to be excluded. Yet heretics provoked closer self-definition, so serving the cause of Christian truth, or at least playing a crucial role in the development of its articulation, even though the orthodox would not have cared to admit it.

Of course, behaviour was not unimportant because the God Christians honoured demanded high moral standards, but the specific ritual demands of the Jewish parent group had been rejected in the process of earlier differentiation, and truth and morality came to be closely associated. Those who believed falsely were assumed also to live badly. Most heretics were attacked not just for their beliefs, but justly or unjustly also on moral grounds; for this was assumed to confirm their heretical attitude. As time went on the demands for uniformity of practice as well as belief became increasingly insistent, and the totalitarianism of Christendom was the result.

The paradox in this is evident in Augustine's thought. The one by whom the Love of God was most deeply appreciated in both mind and heart was the one who set imperial authority on to the Donatists and taught a rigid and uncompromising predestinarianism. A parallel paradox lies in the universal claims of a creed affirming the one God of all the earth being used to exclude multitudes of God's creatures from his providential care and love. Christianity has within it the seeds of a prophetic criticism of its own exclusivism and intolerance. Yet how can it eschew the imperative to grapple with the issue of truth, and counter views of the way things are which are incompatible with its fundamental vision?

Another paradox lies at the heart of the story we have told, namely that it appears to be a process of finer and finer definition to the extent that the precise make-up of the Trinitarian God becomes a matter of contention, and yet it was concern to preserve the mystery of God which produced the definition. God's otherness and infinity was the clinching argument against those neat and simple 'First Cause' definitions which threatened to reduce God to the measure of the human mind. The mystery of the Trinity was the outcome, yet put a step wrong in enunciating that doctrine and you become a heretic!

At least a sophisticated theology of this kind could not fall into the trap of arguing from a supposedly personal God to a male idol. One positive feature of the feminist critique of Christian theology is that it exposes the limitations not only of much popular Christianity but of the theistic traditions of most modern Western philosophy of religion, as does the Trinitarian theology of the Fathers. For they were absolutely clear that anthropomorphism was inappropriate.

True there was a tendency to think of God by analogy with male figures, like fathers and kings and judges, but the correlate of this was the sense that the human persona related to God appropriately as female, the *psychē* (a feminine word) responding as bride to her husband's love – indeed humanity renewed in the *ekklēsia* (another feminine word) sometimes appearing as the bride of Christ, sometimes as symbolized in the person of Mary, the Queen of Heaven. These may be stereotypical views of male and female relations, but they do at least highlight the non-literal nature of the language, for humanity as a whole, men included, are incorporated in Lady Church. In fact, the Fathers repeatedly stated that all sexual connotations were inappropriate when considering the transcendent Being of God, his begetting of his Son or the reality of spiritual marriage. It is of the nature of human language and conceptuality to find itself stretched to breaking point in its attempts to speak of God, otherwise idolatry is the result. This tension is the creative dynamic at the heart of Christian understanding of God.

But that discussion raises another issue. The story we have told is about the refinement of specific doctrines characteristic of Christianity, but we have presented it as a process of community self-definition. If as we suggested at the beginning our own concerns affect the telling of the story, why has the story not grappled with the issue of the Christian identity of women? All the theologians mentioned have been men – where are the Mothers of the Church? and what about the dreadful calumnies these so-called Fathers perpetrated against women, as documented in recent feminist literature?

A responsible historian may in a sense create history, but still cannot change it. That no women were involved in the particular process that produced the creeds is a matter of history that cannot be changed. Relations between men and women are structured by 'symbolic worlds', and the resulting conventional assumptions are deeply embedded in particular societies and cultures. It is not particularly surprising that women were not directly involved in the conflicts that produced the creeds. We may wish to pass judgment on that culture and society, but to do so wholesale is uncritical, and responsible history requires that judgment is balanced by an attempt to enter that world and 'think their thoughts after them'. Furthermore, the much-quoted passages purporting to represent the views of a patriarchal and prejudiced male hierarchy, though certainly offensive, are not necessarily wholly characteristic of the attitudes towards women even of those from whom they are quoted. They can be balanced by many cases of deep pastoral and spiritual relationships in which women contributed to the church's sense of its ideology, both by their vision and their example. But to document that would be to write another book.

There have been feminists who have welcomed the Gnostic literature, suggesting that here we find women liberated, and regretting the development of authority structures in the church which favoured the resurgence of patriarchy. But the Gnostic position was hostile to a proper affirmation of the bodily, and therefore of feminine identity. On the one hand its asceticism encouraged the tendency to 'unsex', and on the other Gnostics affirmed that women had a place either by becoming male or sinking their sexuality in androgyny. Potentially, if not actually, the orthodox refusal to denigrate the material and physical was more favourable to women's identity. It was the insidious tendency for a Platonic-kind of dualism to slip into a gnostic-kind of dualism which failed to prevent misogyny and the phenomenon of transvestite saints when the church developed its own ascetic movement.

Even if most readers have not noticed, women have been there in the story, for there were women martyrs and women saints and even women missionaries and biblical scholars, celebrated in panegyric and hagiography just like the men. Like men, women martyrs and ascetics were 'types' of Christ. Conversely, all alike were believed to have fallen short of the glory of God, all alike were in need of salvation, and as Christ reversed the Fall of Adam, so Mary reversed the Fall of Eve. The specific case of women was not often explicit precisely because these theologians were concerned about the whole human race, and their perspective was universal. The Fathers are less blameworthy for their misogyny than those who have exploited some of their statements in a very different context and with differing intent.

For in this period the primary issue concerned the nature of God conceived as transcendent yet in relationship with the world, the whole cosmos, material and spiritual, the whole of humanity, flesh and spirit. In a profound sense the doctrine of creation undergirds the developed pattern of patristic theology, expressing its grasp of God's gracious being, nature and activity, as well as its perception of the world's contingency and need for saving union with the divine, a union effected in the being, nature and atoning activity of the incarnate Word. I would submit that the questions posed by such a standpoint remain the fundamental theological issues which have to be addressed.

For the final matter to be considered must surely be this: Should the credal productions at the end of this process be treated as determinative of belief today? The temptation is to offer a challenge: what do you think? A full discussion would go far beyond the bounds of this introductory volume, and the discerning reader will have detected the author's standpoint. Suffice it to say this:

On the one hand, any and every attempt at doctrinal definition is bound to be divisive and also mislead limited human minds into imagining that they can encompass the mystery of the divine in a series of propositions couched in human language and concepts. On the other hand, there are issues of truth and identity which matter and which belong to the whole corporate life of the Christian community through history, and which cannot appropriately be decided by discrete free-thinking individuals. It must therefore be the case that rejection or replacement of the traditional forms of creed and patterns of doctrine is improper, even though there is an unavoidable responsibility to interpret and reinterpret as culture and language changes.

Christian theology has to be not a fossil but a living entity. Yet it cannot be worked out *de novo* time and time again, and it is depressing how often the old heresies re-emerge and the old issues have to be re-debated because of the sheer ignorance of many Christians about their own history. Often the most belligerently orthodox are least true to the spirit of classical Christian theology. Understanding the course of argument and entering sympathetically into the issues as they were once discerned, expressed and discussed is a good starting-point for thinking systematically about Christian doctrine in a different cultural context. And this is the responsibility, as far as in them lies, of any who would identify with the Christian community and claim allegiance to the Word made flesh. For response to the Logos of God demands a spirituality which has, not just obedient love, but rationality, integrity and a desire for truth at its very heart.

Time Chart

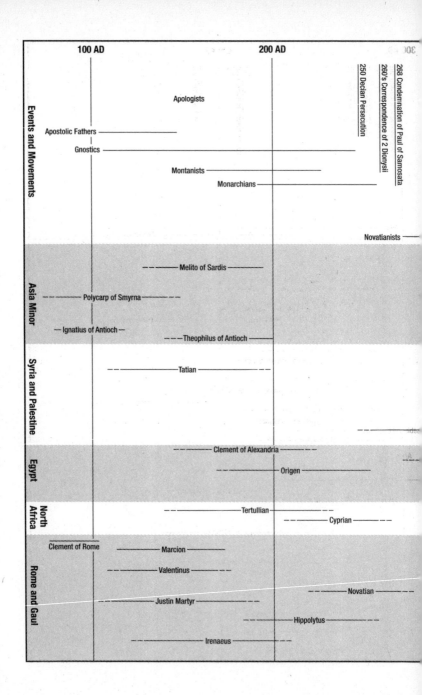

300 AD

400 AD

303 Diocletianic Persecution
308 Constantine in West
320 Constantine in East
325 Council of Nicaea

381 Council of Constantinople

410 Sack of Rome

451 Council of Chalcedon

Arians ———————————————

Donatists ———————————————— Christological controversies

————— Basil of Caesarea ———

————— Gregory of Nazianzus ———————

————— Gregory of Nyssa ——— — —

————— Nemesius of Emesa ———

— — — Nestorius ———————

— — — Eustathius of Antioch ——— — —

— — — John Chrysostom ———

— — Diodore of Tarsus ——— — —

— — Theodore of Mopsuestia ———

————— Theodoret of Cyrus ———

————— Apollinaris of Laodicea ———

— — Epiphanius of Salamis ——— — —

usebius of Caesarea ——— — —

— — — Cyril of Jerusalem ———

Arius

————— Athanasius ———

— — — Cyril of Alexandria———

————— Didymus the Blind ———

————— Augustine of Hippo ———

— — — Pelagius ———

— — ————— Ambrose ———

— — ————— Jerome ———

— — ————— Rufinus ———

————— Hilary of Poitiers ———

Glossary

Achamōth: a corruption of the Hebrew *Hochmah* = Wisdom. A Gnostic name used for the Lesser or Fallen Wisdom born as a result of Sophia's sin.

Anthrōpotokos: Bearer (Mother) of Man. A title used for the Virgin Mary in opposition to Theotokos (see below), emphasizing the humanity of Christ borne by his human mother.

archē : beginning/first principle, or rule/sovereignty.

Bythos : Deep. A title used by Gnostics for the Infinite. Unknowable Forefather.

Christotokos: Bearer (Mother) of Christ.

Decad : a company made up of ten.

Demiurge : craftsman, maker. Used for the Creator God.

Dōdecad : a company made up of twelve.

ek : out of.

en : in.

ecclēsia : assembly, church.

economy : *see below* oikonomia.

energeia : force, action, operation.

episcopos : overseer, superintendent, bishop.

filioque : Latin – and the Son, a Western addition to the Niceno-Constantinopolitan creed.

gnōsis : knowledge.

haeresēs : options, sects, parties, heresies.

homoiousios : of similar/like substance/being.

homoousios : of the same substance/being.

huiopoiēsis : the fashioning of sons, filiation.

hybris : insolence, violence, arising from pride of an inappropriate kind.

hypostasis –ēs (pl.): that which 'stands under', substance, the real nature of a particular.

logikoi : rational beings

logos : word, sentence, argument, reason, order, rationality.

Monad : a single entity.

monarchia : single rule or sovereignty, monarchy, or single first principle, beginning.

nemesis : vengeance, fate.

Ogdoad : a company of eight.

oikonomia : household management. Used theologically to express God's providential arrangements in relation to the world, and later specifically for the incarnation.

plēroma : fullness. A Gnostic term used for the whole divine of spiritual realm peopled by aeons.

prosōpon : face, mask, person.

psychē : soul, life-force.

sacramentum : Latin – oath, later sacrament.

sōma-sēma : body-tomb, a Greek jingle.

Sophia : Wisdom. Personified in the biblical tradition, e.g. Proverbs 8, and developed in Gnostic mythology as the spiritual principle which over-reached herself and caused the creation of the world.

substantia : Latin = hypostasis, substance, that which 'stands under'.

theopoiēsis : divinization or deification, being fashioned into 'gods'.

Theotokos : Bearer (Mother) of God, cf. Anthropotokos.

traditio et redditio : Latin – the handing on and giving back, in other words, the receiving and reciting of a tradition, particularly the creed.

traditor : Latin – one who handed over the scriptures to the persecuting authorities.

treptos : changeable, temptable.

Triad : a company of Three, equivalent to Trinitas (Latin), hence Trinity.

Further Reading

A. There are a number of other useful introductory books which will provide different perspectives on the period:

Henry Chadwick, *The Early Church*, Penguin 1967
Boniface Ramsey, *Beginning to Read the Fathers*, Darton, Longman & Todd 1986
Maurice Wiles, *The Christian Fathers*, SCM Press 1977

B. One important next step is to explore the original texts in translation. To begin with this can be done through the use of anthologies:

For documentary evidence of many kinds, use J. Stevenson, *A New Eusebius*, revised edition by W. H. C. Frend, SPCK 1987 and *Creeds, Councils and Controversies*, also revised edition, SPCK 1989.

To get a sense of broad theological argument over a range of issues, use Maurice Wiles and Mark Santer (eds), *Documents in Early Christian Thought*, Cambridge University Press 1975.

To explore particular themes and issues, the series 'Sources of Early Christian Thought' produced by Fortress Press, Philadelphia, contains useful volumes. Those relevant to the subjects treated in this book are: William Rusch, *The Trinitarian Controversy*, 1980; R. A. Norris Jr, *The Christological Controversy*, 1980; J. Patout Burns, *Theological Anthropology*, 1981; and E. Glenn Hinson, *Understandings of the Church*, 1986. Also of interest are K. Froelich, *Biblical Interpretation in the Early Church*, 1984; Agnes Cunningham, *The Early Church and the State*, 1982; Charles Kannengiesser, *Early Christian Spirituality*, 1986; and Jan Womer, *Morality and Ethics in Early Christianity*, 1987.

Older, but useful, collections of texts are found in T. H. Bindley and F. W. Green (eds), *Ecumenical Documents of the Faith*, Methuen

1950, reissued by Greenwood Press 1987, and the volumes edited by H. Bettenson:

Documents of the Christian Church, Oxford University Press 1943
Early Christian Fathers, Oxford University Press 1956
Later Christian Fathers, Oxford University Press 1970

The more ambitious may wish to sample complete treatises. Penguin Classics contain a number: e.g. *Early Christian Writings*, new edition 1987; Eusebius, *History of the Church*, 1965; Augustine, *Confessions*, 1961 and *City of God*, 1972. The most comprehensive collections are found in the nineteenth-century series 'Ante-Nicene Christian Fathers' and 'Nicene and Post-Nicene Christian Fathers' published by Eerdmans. There are also two recent American series to which additions are constantly being made: 'Ancient Christian Writers' published by Paulist Press and 'Fathers of the Church' from Catholic Universities of America Press. The series 'Oxford Early Christian Texts' (Oxford University Press) and the Loeb Classical Library (Harvard University Press) face the Greek and Latin texts with English translation and include a number of treatises referred to in this introduction. Some others referred to are published in particular editions, e.g. Tertullian, *Adversus Praxeam*, edited and translated by E. Evans, SPCK 1948.

Also significant is the gnostic literature now available. Again anthologies like those of R. M. Grant (*Gnosticism: An Anthology*, Collins 1961) and W. Foerster (*Gnosis*, 2 vols, translated R. McL. Wilson, Oxford 1972, 1974) may provide a starting point, especially as they include some of the patristic evidence, as well as a selection of rediscovered texts. Access to the latter is provided by Bentley Layton (ed) *The Gnostic Scriptures*, Doubleday and SCM Press 1988; some readers may like to tackle James Robinson (ed), *The Nag Hammadi Library in English*, Brill, third revised edition 1988.

C. Initial suggestions for more advanced or specialized readings:

J. N. D. Kelly, *Early Christian Doctrines*, A. & C. Black, fifth edition 1977
J. N. D. Kelly, *Early Christian Creeds*, Longman, third edition 1972
J. Quasten, *Patrology* (three volumes, reference), Spectrum, Christian Classics 1983

Frances Young, *From Nicaea to Chalcedon*, SCM Press and Fortress Press 1983

Robin Lane Fox, *Pagans and Christians*, 1986, Penguin 1988

Kurt Rudolph, *Gnosis*, T. & T. Clark 1984

Hans von Campenhausen, *The Formation of the Christian Bible*, Fortress 1977

R. M. Grant, *Gnosticism and Early Christianity*, Harper & Row and Oxford University Press 1959

R. M. Grant, *Greek Apologists of the Second Century*, Westminster Press and SCM Press 1988

H. Chadwick, *Early Christian Thought and the Classical Tradition*, Oxford University Press 1966

L. W. Barnard, *Justin Martyr*, Cambridge University Press 1967

R. A. Norris, *God and World in Early Christianity*, A. & C. Black 1966

J. Trigg, *Origen*, John Knox and SCM Press 1983

H. Crouzel, *Origen*, English translation, T. & T. Clark 1989

W. H. C. Frend, *The Donatist Church*, Oxford University Press 1952

A. Grillmeier, *Christ in Christian Tradition*, Volume 1, Mowbray and John Knox, second revised edition 1975

R. P. C. Hanson, *The Search for the Early Christian Understanding of God*, T. & T. Clark 1988

Rowan Williams, *Arius: Heresy and Tradition*, Darton, Longman & Todd 1987

Peter Brown, *Augustine of Hippo*, Faber 1967

Peter Brown, *The Body and Society*, Columbia University Press 1988 and Faber 1989

G. L. Prestige, *God in Patristic Thought*, SPCK 1936

T. F. Torrance, *The Trinitarian Faith*, T. & T. Clark 1988

Stuart G. Hall, *Doctrine and Practice in the Early Church*, SPCK 1991

Ian Hazlett, *Early Christian Origins and Evolution to AD 600*, SPCK 1991

Index